The Fire at Massie's Bakery

The Fire at Massie's Bakery

An East End Family's Journey

Charles Smith

Published by Jeremy Mills Publishing Limited
on behalf of Charles Smith
www.jeremymillspublishing.co.uk

This edition first published 2011

ISBN 978-1905217-07-6

A CIP catalogue record for this book is available from the
British Library

Typeset in Monotype Bembo by Concept
Printed in the UK

Contents

Foreword

It was sometime in the late 1990s; I had boarded the Emirates plane out of Heathrow's Terminal 3 after being chauffeured to the airport in an airline courtesy limo and idling for an hour in the comfy armchairs of the airline business lounge overlooking the swanky shops while reading *The Sunday Times* and sipping a G&T. All was predictably normal and very routine to the point of boredom. I had done this journey a hundred times; though it felt like a thousand. It was, like many thousands of other London commuters, just the regular 'trudge to the office'. It was just that my office was 3,000 miles away in Abu Dhabi. Phil Collins' hit *Another Day in Paradise* always rung in my head for some bizarre reason on these flights; an ironic parody of the fact that I was actually 'getting back to the grindstone' to coin a phrase from my ancestral roots. But this particular journey was to be different; it was to be the start of an entirely different journey altogether; a journey into my family's past; its roots, its trials and finally its emergence from the grime and grindstone of London's infamous early twentieth-century East End.

On that day I carried with me a bundle of typed papers; a collection of my father's thoughts and memories now that he was retired and had time to idle in 'God's waiting room'. My dad had bought himself an electronic typewriter and I had encouraged him to record some of those '. . . I remember the time when . . .' stories that all parents relate to their children. Little did I know that he would apply himself so doggedly to the task that by the time of this flight to Abu Dhabi, I was clutching a very large wad of papers indeed.

I settled into my comfy business class seat. I sat back and pulled out the bundle of papers, and started to read. Little did I expect the detailed insight into my family's life that was to unfurl. My father had been an engineer all his life and thankfully for an engineer, he was a great creative writer; he'd written plays and even musicals which had been performed on the stage by local dramatic groups to widespread acclaim. But this was to be his masterpiece. Very quickly I was totally enthralled by the story emerging; a young boy, a dominant step father, escape, flight (on foot), an epic sea journey to Australia, crime, grime, war, peace, death and finally economic boom. It was all there and though I did not feature, it was in essence all about me or rather all about the trials and tribulations of my forebears.

I read the assorted manuscripts with increasing interest as the characters began to unfold, pausing only occasionally to fix a distant stare out of the window at 37,000 feet onto some distant land far below or onto some fluffy clouds in the distance, to reflect upon my dad's writings. I tried to imagine the struggle of daily life, the stench and the grime, the harsh discipline of the Victorian era, the wondrous sights on the journey to Australia, the horrors of nightly bombing, being bombed out of house and home, sharing with the in-laws, but of course I couldn't *really* imagine. It was impossible unless you had actually experienced it yourself, but this collection of memories was more than just the usual anecdotes related by all fathers to their sons along the lines 'I remember . . .'. This was *my* family's story and a book in the making.

After an unusually enthralling seven hours the aircraft landed in Abu Dhabi and I was whisked away in another limo to my 26th floor apartment over-looking the beautiful blue waters of the Arabian Gulf on Abu Dhabi's Corniche. That bloody tune was still playing on a loop somewhere in the back of my mind but now I appreciated it and my privileged life a whole lot more; I *was* truly in a 'relative' paradise. I determined there and then to get my dad to pull this loose collection of recollections together into a chronologically ordered work starting with John Maudesley, my great grandfather who sadly I can only now recall, laid out in his coffin in the parlour, on the day of his funeral when I was just six.

'Dad, why don't you reorganize those papers you gave me?'

'What papers?' came his reply.

'You know that collection of stories you bought that typewriter for?'

'Aw I don't know; I never meant them to be anything more than a few thoughts for you when I'm gone.'

'They are really very interesting and witty you know'.

'Really?'

'Yes! They just need a little reorganization, you know chronologically . . .' and then adding with my marketers head on, '. . . and a few photos would not go amiss too!'

And so started another epic journey for the Smith family; nearly a decade later the publishing of this book! My dad did what I asked him, painstakingly typing and retyping his recollections on his electronic typewriter. I could never get him onto a PC and the benefits of 'cut n paste' so this book is all the more a true labour of love for us both, being a very small task in comparison to the daily traumas of the life of my great grandfather, grandfather and father in all that they had laboured over in order to get my backside in that comfy business class seat to Abu Dhabi!

In editing but mainly in the long moments of quiet reflection in the serenity of the garden of my now embarrassingly palatial company villa in Qatar, I realized how grateful I should be for *another day in paradise*! I also realized with almost distressing unease, how much our world had changed in the generations between my great grandfather and I. The family had indeed been on a long journey. Not only were there the striking differences in lifestyles but there were odd interesting facts such our family's interest in travel. I just do mine in the comfort of a modern airline whilst both my great grandfathers and grandfathers did their intercontinental journeys in old square-riggers and later tramp steamers, taking months to achieve what I regularly do in hours . . . and complain bitterly about! I was shocked to read that my dad had miraculously avoided death but then had to stare it in the face in its most grotesque rendition, when still only a boy during a rocket attack on London during World War Two. I also discovered why I was so interested in the fire in the open hearth of my grandmother's house; it was in the genes as you will read in this book. But ours is not the story of some special family; its just the tale of an ordinary family experiencing what some have said are extraordinary times and developments. The difference is that, thankfully, my dad captured it for us all and for that I am truly indebted and profoundly grateful.

Perry Smith
A very proud and humbled son.

Introduction

The Maudesley Connection

It is an old English adage that – 'One can choose one's friends but one cannot choose one's relations!' Throughout life I have always been lucky in the choice of my friends but I have to admit that in respect of my relations I had no choice but had to rely on fate. But even in this 'out of my hands' responsibility, I have been oh! so lucky. I have explained in later sections how I came to be closer to my maternal family – the Maudesleys, by living in the same Canning Town street and being virtually raised by my grandparents as my mother strove to supplement my sea-going father's poor wages by working as a waitress before buying and selling goods on a 'small profit, quick return' basis.

The logistical nightmare of raising eleven children in a small three bedroom East End of London terraced house, throughout the harsh times of the First World War and the economic depression of the twenties, only my grandparents and God must have known how they provided me with the best child care I could ever have had with love and genuine affection as their first grandson.

It was a strict but fair home environment with high moral values that my mother had severely tested by accidentally (I think?) sullying that moral high ground and bringing the community shame to fall upon her and the family by 'being with child', but even more fearfully shame upon the 'respectable Maudesleys'. The double edged sword of my grandparents wrath may have hovered momentarily over my distressed mum's head but never did the blade of blame fall upon me to also be unwanted as I found over the ensuing years in their care, that John and Kate Maudesley were the best grandparents in the world. They proved to be the perfect role models upon whose principles the ensuing years of my long life were based. They were also very proud that, in my grandfather's case, it bordered on stubborness as he often found it hard to forgive even the slightest misdemeanour or apologise if he was in the wrong. He was a strong character and a disciplinarian but, fortunately, administered it orally, rather than physically, with his stern scouse accent that could never be questioned. On the other hand, Grandmother Maudesley had the countenance of a formidable lady (i.e. 'battle-axe') who could administer a silent admonishing glare to anyone who annoyed her and guaranteed to 'freeze' any wrongdoer in their tracks! I must admit that I soon learned that 'silence was golden' as I became both aware and afraid of upsetting her and the resultant whack on the head with a wooden spoon. *If* I was going to be naughty I did my best to stay out of her arms at reach, especially if she was rolling pastry and my knowledge that the rolling pin was the difference between a fractured skull and a bruise on the head caused by the wooden spoon.

Both grandparents were hard workers and instilled this characteristic in all their family with the saying that 'Idle hands make work for the devil!'. Grandfather was a man of experience rather than of education so that he encouraged every one of his children to learn first, learn fast and then get a trade. The many hours that I spent in his company helped me in so many ways to mould me from my infancy to being who I now am. His rather quick temper often camouflaged the real loveable softie that I knew and his 'keeping himself to himself' was interpreted by many as his being aloof whereas his sole attention was focused on his family responsibilities. Grandmother, with a large family to clothe and feed, worked tirelessly in the home by cleaning, cooking and making clothes for them all and yet still finding time to take in washing and ironing to help pay the bills. Of the eleven children, I can remember the eight, who survived to witness my introduction as the first grandson of the Maudesleys, all of them being completely different to each other either in their chosen career fields or in their facial similarities or physiques but all of them alike as they remain locked into my long term memory.

I am so glad that by some quirk of fate I became an integral part of the Maudesley family and was able to witness and to share through thick and thin, the good times and the not so good times in their life. Alas those times relentlessly marched on and, one-by-one, their lives have been claimed either through natural causes or, in some cases, through tragic accidents. The youngest family member passed away in 2003 so ending seventy-five years of the privilege of my being part of the Maudesley dynasty. I now look back on the paper chains that originally led to that three quarters of a century deep association but are now, in my mind, chains forged from the finest steel that can never be broken. The following pages will reveal what part those paper chains played in the establishment of the Maudesley family settling in the docklands area of London's East End and for which I for one, shall be forever grateful.

Charles Smith

The author as President, Bexley Probus Club, 1996–7

CHAPTER ONE

Christmas 1890 – Fire and Flight

As a child, I asked my mother why our house and that of my grandmother and grandfather never had Christmas decorations adorning the living room. The answer, I found, lay in Liverpool's Bootle dock area where my grandfather, Mr John Maudesley was brought up.

He lived in a two–up and two–down dockworker's terraced house that he shared with his early-widowed mother and his sister Mary-Ellen. His father died before he had reached his teens, his premature death being blamed upon the heavy manual work he undertook in order to earn a living. It came as a shock when, during his early teens, his mother told him that the family were moving to a bigger and better house, next door to Massie's Bakery. However, the pleasing news was tempered by her explaining that she was going to remarry – to Mr Massie, the baker.

George Massie was a tall, elegant man with a regal beard but his stern features could not be disguised. His bakery was a thriving business catering for the needs of local dockworkers and their families.

A week before his first Christmas under old man Massie's roof, while his mother and stepfather were out for the evening, my grandfather took it upon himself to decorate the house with home-made paper chains; an act that was to shape the rest of his life and the future of the whole family.

That same evening, only the shouts of the on-duty baker, working through the night to ensure hot, fresh produce for early workers and local customers, saved my grandfather's family from complete disaster.

The baker had slipped out from the heat of the bakery for a quick smoke. In the cool night air, he could still feel the heat from inside. Sweat poured off his brow onto his white baker's coat, leaking down his face and staining his collar. It was almost overpowering. Had it been this hot before?

Then he noticed.

Through the downstairs window of the living room, flames were licking up the wall from the fallen paper chains.

The duty-baker raised the alarm. Panic ensued. The family, shaken awake from hard-earned sleep, leapt around, each one responding in their own, frantic way.

Mother hurled armfuls of clothes and belongings from the windows whilst Stepfather yelled, red-faced. The Daughter cried through thickening smoke

Mr George Massie circa 1895.

*Mr George Massie and Mrs Massie
(formerly Maudesley).*

and stinging eyes and the Son, my grandfather, was motionless, consumed with fear.

The baker managed to push them out into the refuge of the street, breathing heavily, flustered and hot. They stood and stared at the fire in total disbelief. The building lit up like a giant pinwheel, spitting out ash and decorating the pavement with hot snow. Neighbours soon joined them to watch, helpless, as the fire took hold.

Unfortunately for my grandfather, the duty-baker spilt-the-beans to his guv'nor, Mr Massie, and told him what he had seen through the window. They speculated on what had caused the fire – it was the paper chains! The very same paper chains which my grandfather had carelessly hung from the fireplace that evening despite the stern warnings of his fire-conscious step-father.

In full view of the gathering crowd amidst the raging fire, my grandfather was humiliatingly punished, first by his mother, then by George Massie himself. He was punched, slapped, and berated, and all the while, their livelihood was being reduced to ruins.

I can imagine my grandfather wanting nothing more than to get out of there as quick as his holed boots could carry him. He was feeling sorry for himself as well as thoroughly ashamed, and now the guilt, the slaps and the fire itself, were beginning to burn his face.

He gathered up as many of his belongings as he could, plus those that his mother had thrown from the bedroom window in her panic, and in the commotion, slipped quietly away. His parents and sister had turned their attention back to the raging fire and in the pandemonium had not noticed him leaving until it was too late.

With the threatening last words of George Massie still ringing in his ears, 'You'll pay for this me-lad!', an escape plan began to form in his young mind. His first thought that dreadful night was to get far away as quickly as he could, to save him from the further punishments that would surely follow.

As he half ran and half walked towards the Mersey docks he toyed with the idea of running away to sea. He envisaged long nights aboard big ships with hard men and strong drinks. But that was too obvious a plan, and it would be the first place his stepfather would look for him.

He pondered heading northwards. He could easily like the North – colder, cheaper, more nooks and crannies in which to hide. Taking flight north? But to where? Scotland?

On that bitterly cold, damp and foggy night the eerie stillness of the dock road was broken only by the mournful sounds of foghorns from ships large and small, sailing on the River Mersey.

To an offending sixteen year old on the run it must have been traumatic. His mind must have turned over and over. What to do next? Where to go? Knowing he had done wrong, albeit accidentally, he wondered if he would ever return home or see his mother and sister again.

Clutching his small bundle of belongings, he must have looked like Oliver Twist. To keep at least one hand warm and reassure himself the little money he had was safe, he nestled his hand in his trouser pocket, a few coppers the sum total of his worldly wealth.

As he headed along the nearby Regent Road and, thankfully, away from Bootle, he judged his progress by the number of dock gates he passed until finally he was clear of the docks and on the Crosby Road. He reckoned he could be in Southport before dawn and figured he could sleep in one of the seaside public shelters. They reminded him of the time his mother took him and his sister there, just after their father had died.

En-route to Southport, he passed through the area known as Seaforth. This provoked a memory of something he'd read, or heard about – the 'Seaforth Highlanders', a Scottish Regiment.

Scotland?

Surely old man Massie wouldn't think of looking for him up there? He wouldn't trudge through the north, sniffing out a fire-starter like a hound sniffs out a fox.

At that moment it was decided. He would try and join the Seaforth Highlanders; hide out, scrape a living for himself and maybe even grow to like it. Who knew?

With the enormity of what he'd done fading into the night, he continued his march northwards.

Although my grandfather could not (or did not want to) recall much of his trek northwards, he reckoned it took him the best part of a week by way of the less busy coastal roads, so as to avoid going inland through the industrial areas of Lancashire. He slept rough but managed to keep going by spending little and scrounging much, through lifts and food along the way and telling the odd fib or two, until he reached the Scottish border and then onwards to Glasgow. As if the dingy back streets in which he found himself were not enough to deepen his gloom, he was cold, very hungry, dog tired and feeling sorry for himself. Whilst turning over in his mind the circumstances which had led him to this foreboding dark Victorian city he felt increasingly lonely.

Christmas was nigh and he missed his mother and sister at home in Bootle. He felt like crying, even marching back and facing the considerable wrath of old man Massie. However, at that moment, salvation appeared in the form of an Army Recruiting Office. His earlier original idea to become a 'Seaforth Highlander' resurfaced and became all the more appealing as he visualised a warm bed, food and a bath. He needed no pushing up the steps to face the burly recruiting sergeant.

Disappointingly, the office was not for the 'Seaforth Highlanders' but a sister regiment, the 'Argyll and Sutherland Highlanders', reputed along with the 'Black Watch', to be Scotland's premier infantry regiment. While he tried to collect his muddled thoughts, his eyes alighted on a large portrait of a soldier in full ceremonial dress, complete with kilt, sporran and bearskin 'busby' hat. To my grandfather, at that time, one Highlander was just the same as another so he signed up for a short-term engagement.

He was well aware of the Regiment's minimum age requirement of seventeen, but he lied about his date of birth and, with no telltale identification document, claimed to be an orphan. This was good enough for the Recruiting Officer.

Grandfather entered the 'Argylls' as a Private and subsequently completed a rigorous basic training programme before being allowed to officially don the full military regalia of the Regiment.

After undergoing the intensive training expected of a Scottish Highlander to equip him for the military life ahead of him, my grandfather settled down to regimental routine comprising of guard duties and ceremonial parades, a significant change from his Bootle days. He was still haunted by the memory of the fire and running away from the wrath of his mother and step-father, but now he felt confident and able to look after himself and he soon relished the prospect of his first overseas posting. A posting, perhaps, to the warmer climes of India or Africa, away from the cold barracks of the 'Argylls' and guard duties, exposed to the bitter winds of a long Scottish winter.

Sometime during this transitional stage, having completed his training and feeling secure in the knowledge that he was safe from discovery, came the moment which my grandfather had dreaded since he walked into that recruiting office – a summons from the Regimental Sergeant Major.

Militarily, he hadn't put a foot wrong, so he knew that it could mean only one thing. His closely guarded secret about his disappearance and whereabouts had been discovered. He hadn't to wait too long to be marched by the Orderly Sergeant into the Regimental Sergeant Major's office where he was met by the angry, stern eyes of his glowering stepfather.

George Massie who, at not inconsiderable expense, had tracked him down, and had secured his release from the Army due to his being under military age.

'Highlander' John Maudesley of the Argyll and Sutherland Highlanders Regiment, circa 1891.

Mr Massie now made it clear to this 'ungrateful wretch of a stepson' that if it had been left to him, he could have rotted in Glasgow or India, or anywhere else for that matter! But it was his mother who worried and fretted over her only son's absence and so had instigated the search that ended with my grandfather unceremoniously departing from the 'Argyll's' barracks and being taken back to Bootle and the rebuilt Massie's Bakery.

CHAPTER TWO

Running Away – To Sea and Australia

What threats and recriminations were meted out when my grandfather arrived back home are unknown. Suffice it to say the old man Massie versus young John Maudesley situation was untenable. Grandfather took the first opportunity to flee from the memories of the fire, and from his seemingly unforgiving family.

Early in 1892, he walked down to Bootle docks. Several ships of varying shapes and sizes, from small dirty tramp steamers to large ocean-going passenger ships, bobbed quietly in the dock. Grandfather admired them all. He let his eyes wander down the line of well-crafted vessels and already his heart thumped with excitement.

And then he saw it, rocking slowly with a majestic elegance that left his heart in his mouth. It was a three-mast square-rigged merchant ship with an imposing bow figurehead and neat white sails. Grandfather was smitten and his heart raced when he saw a cabin boy vacancy pinned to the gangplank. A notice on the other side read 'Sailing at 6.00 am on Wednesday'.

Grandfather couldn't believe his luck. A new, foolproof escape plan, with pay! The sudden realisation that the ship was sailing the very next day propelled him up the ramp and into the burly figure of the Bosun. He enquired about the vacancy and apart from name and age, no other questions were asked. He signed on the dotted line and became contracted to complete a round voyage to Australia. Old man Massie would be out of sight and out of mind before he could tie a sailors knot!

That type of ship was popular at the time for undertaking long voyages without the need to refuel, especially across vast oceans like the Indian and Pacific, where winds would hurtle them along at a great rate of knots. They were known as Clipper ships and were used almost exclusively on the India, Australia and New Zealand runs. They departed with British manufactured goods onboard, the type of solid engineered goods you still find to this day scattered across the far-flung corners of the former British Empire, enjoying it's heyday in my grandfather's day. They returned with wool, cotton, silks, and spices from the East. Whilst it is uncertain whether the ship was steam assisted or relied solely on the trade winds, the round trip was to take about a year.

Conditions on board, for a nineteenth century maiden voyage cabin boy were, to say the least, poor. Treatment handed out to the deck-boys (as they were called once the ship set sail) was both terrifying and brutal. It caused my Grandfather and another newly signed-on deck-boy to choose to spend their off-duty times in the ship's rope locker with rats and creepy-crawlies rather than share their companionship with the drunken sailors.

The other cabin boy hailed from Birkenhead and had been a farm labourer and Jack-of-all-trades before starting his sea-going life. He had experienced only short runs to Ireland and this was his first long voyage.

During their brief span of friendship Mick (as I shall call him) revealed himself as a real man-of-the-world and taught my grandfather how to splice and whip a rope end, spit downwind, and make tobacco from rum-soaked leaves.

Deck-boys were little more than dogsbodies. They cleaned the ship's brass and swabbed decks whilst being generally harassed by the bullying crew. For days the two young boys were racked with such severe seasickness that neither of them could eat and what little did pass their lips was soon on the way up again. Some of the crew cruelly suggested drinking seawater as a means of curbing the nausea. My grandfather was living almost solely on salt beef and hard biscuit. The seemingly endless gale-force winds and heavy seas left him in a constant state of seasickness until a more sympathetic crewman spotted him drinking seawater in pursuit of relief and told him that was the worst thing possible.

They reached the west coast of Africa and crossed the Equator. Both the lads were unanimous in their most fervent wish – that the ship would be wrecked so they might have a chance of getting ashore, even if it was only a desert island. Anything seemed better than this hell on the high seas. Both were natural targets for teasing in addition to the bullying. They were subjected to a number of cruel practical jokes but eventually the Bosun intervened and admonished the seamen responsible.

By the time they reached Perth in Western Australia, they had been at sea for almost six months and both the deck-boys looked weak and emaciated from seasickness and associated loss of appetite. It was whilst coming into Perth that Mick and my grandfather decided this was the time to make a run for it. Unfortunately for them, the sailor on watch spotted them and they were consequently punished by the Bosun.

The ship then sailed around the southern coast of Australia towards Sydney. Hurt but undeterred they could only hope they would be allowed ashore. In an effort to earn the Bosun's trust and gain reward by way of shore leave, they strove to impress with their reformation to obedience and exemplary behaviour.

Following their foiled escape the two friends were kept under constant surveillance by a couple of old sailors and were constantly reminded of their fate should they attempt to escape en-route to Sydney. Any thoughts of jumping overboard and swimming for it were dispelled by gruesome tales of man-eating sharks and giant octopuses.

It was a very hot Saturday morning when the ship moored in Sydney. The crew were given just a few short hours shore leave before the laborious task of unloading the British cargo and loading bales of wool from the outback sheep stations. The completion of the whole operation was scheduled to take the rest of the week. Unfortunately the lads were unaware of that fact.

The shipping company's policy of withholding a large portion of the crew's wages until they signed-off in Liverpool, was to dissuade crewmembers from jumping ship as well as maintaining a degree of control over their behaviour whilst on and off shore. The more experienced sailors however, had the foresight to ensure that they always had a few bob in their pockets to enjoy whatever port of call they found themselves in. The majority of the crew departed the ship quickly leaving the two lads on board doing menial tasks. When darkness began to fall they locked themselves in their rope locker refuge away from the sailors making their noisy, drunken return.

The following day, Sunday, the boys were astonished to be roused from their hideaway by the Bosun who told them that they were being allowed ashore for good behaviour, and because it was the Sabbath. However, it was only on the strict understanding they took no money with them, they were dressed smart and they would be under the guardianship of the notorious Bosun's Mate, a bully, womaniser and drunkard.

Hardly able to believe their luck, they walked down the gangplank and off the ship for the first time in six months, closely followed by their hated guardian. The Bosun's mate pushed his unwilling charges before him determined to bypass a preaching clergyman whose eyes made a beeline for them. They were stopped in their tracks by a Bible-filled hand and a plea for them to renounce their sins.

The clergyman wore a flat pastoral hat, a dog collar and knee-high leather gaiters. In one hand he held the bible whilst the other gripped tightly to the reins of a scruffy horse standing mournfully in the shafts of a passenger cart which had the name of the church mission painted on the side.

The rest of the crew were flocking out of pubs and into the street, determined to satisfy their long overdue frustrations at the local brothels. The Bosun's mate was torn between his allocated duty and his temptation to follow the other carefree sailors. The prospect of going to some church hall to sing hymns and drink weak tea caused him to give in. He surrendered the boys to the temporary care of the clergyman but not before he roughly grabbed the lads and, with a stern expression on his pock-marked face, said, 'Listen to what Father 'Wotsit' here tells you and don't dare mention that I let you out of my sight for even one minute or else you'll both be in serious trouble!' The boys joyfully climbed up on the cart and sat on the front bench, revelling in their good fortune. They waved goodbye, with childlike innocence, to the Bosun's mate.

As their young minds toyed with the idea of escape, the cart was quickly filled with down-and-out characters who were probably too short of money to enjoy the Sydney 'fleshpots' and were in need of a free meal.

'Father Up', as grandfather called him, climbed up onto the seat next to the boys and gave my grandfather his well-worn bible to hold until they reached the Mission. The journey was uncomfortable and very dusty but his mind concentrated on how to get away from that dreaded ship. He didn't know how far from the docks they travelled before the tiring horse was mercifully pulled up outside an old, corrugated iron building that was badly in need of a lick of paint.

In their boyish dreams, stirred since their first sight of Australia and tales of riches waiting to be had, they had envisaged a prosperous life in goldfields, sheep shearing or even going 'walkabouts' in the outback picking up jobs here and there – anything, so long as they could make a quick fortune and return to England in style. There, standing outside the rundown, rusted old church, those dreams were floating further and further away.

In the short walk from the cart to the hut, Mick and grandfather hastily conferred on what to do next. First priority was to fill both themselves and their pockets with as much free food as possible then wait for an opportunity to make a run for it.

Once inside the Mission, a bucket of tea was produced and all new arrivals were given a well-worn, chipped enamel mug. This was followed by a tray of sandwiches and homemade cakes. Although the long-awaited treats were greatly appreciated, the friend's minds were firmly fixed on escape.

The chance to run was unexpectedly presented to them when one of the other rescued inhabitants knocked over a full tea bucket. During the ensuing confusion, they managed to quietly slip out. Bursting through the ramshackle doors and into a sun-filled wilderness, they had never felt so hot.

They ran and ran until they were well clear of the Mission. The feeling of freedom pulsed through their hearts. They let their seafaring legs carry them with no clue as to where they were or what direction they were heading. But they didn't care. They were away from the ship and its brutal crew and now all they could think about was new adventure.

For two days and two very cold nights, they trudged northwards, away from the sea and into the outback. They were getting hungrier, thirstier and hotter by the minute. By their calculations it was January. Grandfather wiped his brow with the back of his hand and exclaimed, 'If this is winter I would hate to be here in the summer!' Neither of them had known of the climatic differences between Australia and England.

On the third morning of their travels they came across a farm. With their free Mission food long since gone, they decided to approach it and offer to work in return for food and drink. Whilst heading toward the farm they were startled by squawking chickens, flapping their wings in anticipation of the boy's approach. They were fat and round and it seemed as if they were crying out to be eaten. This presented itself as too good an opportunity to miss and Mick seized his chance. He crawled slowly across the hard and dusty ground before diving at one unfortunate bird, grabbing it close to him and displaying all his early farm worker skills. Before my grandfather had time to see what was happening, Mick had wrung its neck in one swift movement.

They stole away with their prize, smug and excited at the prospect of real food. After collecting some brushwood and twigs they somehow managed to get a small fire going. Then, Mick prepared their catch. The chicken was skewered with a long stick propped at either end on to a forked branch and, in true barbecue style, was left to cook over the fire.

Unfortunately the boys had not foreseen the repercussions of their fire. The smoke that was created on lighting it was exacerbated by the addition of the chicken's feathers, and this attracted the attention of the farmer's wife who alerted her husband to what she feared was a bush fire. She, her husband, and some of his farm workers, hurried to the scene and doused the flames before lambasting the cowering lads for their reckless act and disregard for the bush.

Under the leadership of the farmer and his wife, the farm workers took great delight in humiliating the chicken thieves. They were locked in the seemingly impregnable chicken house, subjected to chicken-like imitations and had corn thrown at them. This prison was worse than the ship and they wondered how long they would be held there.

As the heat of the day subsided and darkness began to fall, the farmer's wife brought them food and water and told them that the police had been informed. This looming threat and the sound of the clucking chickens meant they hardly got any sleep that night. My grandfather sat there for hours reflecting on how, yet again, a fire was the cause of his problems.

The boys were cooped up for days before the police arrived, with barely enough room to stretch their cramped legs. This time escape was impossible. They were constantly watched over by a fierce looking dog which growled deeply whenever they attempted to move around inside. Relief eventually arrived in the form of the local Bobby who took them into his custody. Glad to escape the smell, the overpowering heat and the confines of their prison, they readily confessed everything.

The prisoners were bundled onto a small horse drawn cart and placed back-to-back with a looped rope around their midriffs, tied to the driving bench. They were forbidden to talk and despite the calls of nature and their extreme discomfort, they were driven down a potholed road for almost four hours under the blazing sun. Any attempt to speak to the constable was silenced when he told them how lucky they were not to have been lynched at the farm.

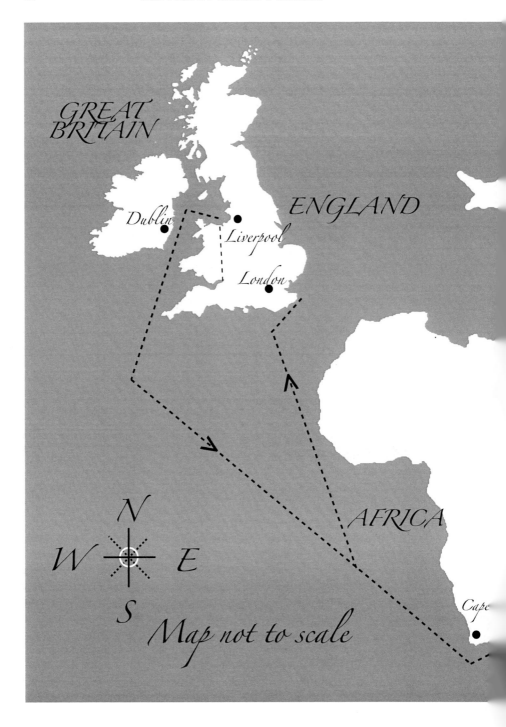

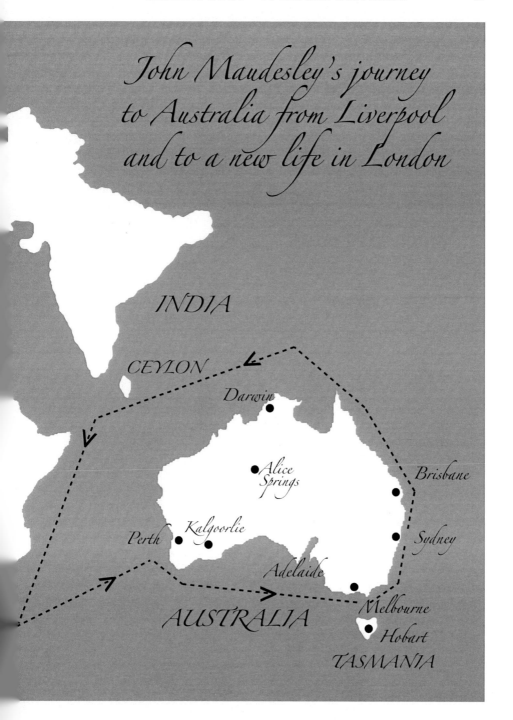

John Maudesley's journey
to Australia from Liverpool
and to a new life in London

INDIA

CEYLON

Darwin

Alice
Springs

Brisbane

Perth   Kalgoorlie

Sydney

Adelaide

AUSTRALIA

Melbourne

Hobart

TASMANIA

The Police Station was actually the policeman's own house and upon arrival the boys were dragged from the cart and locked up in a small windowless room while he made enquiries. They could have been charged with local trespass, stealing, vagrancy or even lighting a prohibited bonfire, but their crime of jumping ship was considered an even more serious offence, with a punishment of their Captain's choice. The lads were convinced that this threat was unenforceable as, by now, their ship would be well on its way to Brisbane, en-route to Ceylon, so they would be out of the reach of their feared Captain. How wrong they were.

A couple of days later they were on the road once more in the constable's horse and cart, back to Sydney docks. As it edged around a corner they met with a sight that perished their souls. Their ship was still tied up in the dock and had just completed loading. A glowering Bosun's mate threw them roughly on board and treated them little better than animals for the remainder of the trip.

For their flagrant disregard of orders and consequent punishment, the lads were hauled before the ship's Captain by the Bosun. They were made to wait for what seemed like hours, until the bellow of a gruff voice was heard to command, 'Bring 'em in Bosun!' The Captain looked up from the papers he was reading and glared at them, slowly shaking his head in disbelief. They must have appeared a sorry spectacle, with their dishevelled appearance, standing unclean and unfed before the Captain, awaiting him to speak. He told them they had jeopardised the safety of the ship and its crew by their childish action of deserting before being officially signed-off. Jumping ship was considered to be a mutinous act and, in the past, punishable by death. The deserters were petrified. What fate would befall them?

The Captain announced that as it was their first trip and since they had been allowed to roam under permission of the Bosun's mate, they would now be returned to his guardianship for the rest of the voyage. Suspecting that he would have been punished for his misdeed and knowing he would be out for revenge, they begged the Captain for mercy, but to no avail. He ordered the Bosun to take them below to give them a good scrub and some hard biscuit for a few days.

The rope locker refuge they had occupied on the outward trip, was now out-of-bounds to them so they were relocated to a small windowless, airless room, not much bigger than one of the large cupboards at Massie's bakery. The heat and smell from the holds, full of Australian wool, made day-to-day living almost unbearable. Their misery was compounded by the heavy work-load and beltings from the unforgiving Bosun's mate.

Although they still discussed escape, it was readily dismissed as a solution to their problems. They had learnt by now that the consequences of failure were severe. Furthermore they were guarded whenever a coastline came into sight so even if they'd wanted to swim for it, they couldn't.

My grandfather did not elaborate any further on his return voyage and was reluctant to go into detail of how they were forcibly kept in their place until the ship's arrival in the London docks, where it was to offload some of the goods before continuing en-route to Liverpool, where the wool would be unloaded and sent to the Lancashire mills. I never did find out whether the ship retraced its outward route, via the Cape of Good Hope and up the west coast of Africa. But one thing is certain – it was a hellish journey.

The ship finally approached England and my grandfather, his mind and body scarred by his first seagoing experience, realised he had no wish to stay on board until it reached Liverpool. Neither did he want to face his stepfather. As they sauntered up the Thames Estuary he carefully weighed the pros and the cons of returning to Bootle and, despite the bond between him and his mother and young sister, who he had missed terribly, he decided to 'sign-off' with only a fraction of the wages due to him because of his bad seagoing record. He reckoned it was a small price to pay for freedom.

Following the docking of the ship in the Victoria Dock (later to be renamed Royal Victoria Dock), grandfather bade a sad and reluctant farewell to Mick, his only close companion for the last year, who had shared his hardships. Mick wanted to return to his hometown of Birkenhead. They shook hands before embracing for just a moment. Although they both said they would write to each other, they walked away knowing they probably never would.

My grandfather had arrived in the East End of London, to an uncertain future, but one away from the beatings of the Bosun's Mate and the chastisement of 'old man Massie'.

CHAPTER THREE

Out of the Pan, into the Fire – Unplanned Arrival

With a hint of apprehension, my grandfather ventured out through the dock gates not knowing which part of London he was in or where he was going. He wandered through the streets of Silvertown, Tidal Basin and Custom House, so reminiscent of his native Bootle docklands area and became immediately aware that he was in a poor, sad area. It cried out so desperately for work, he could almost hear it.

For my grandfather, with his Bootle Docks background, arriving in the East End docklands must have seemed to him like jumping out of the frying pan and into the fire. I, of course, knew no better, having been born into it and did not realise in my childhood that there was life beyond the bounds of the tightly packed terraced housing that characterised Canning Town – named after the canning factories that abounded in the late Victorian era.

Around 150 years ago, the Thames-side of West Ham (now known as Newham) was mainly agricultural and marshland, lying on the east bank of the River Lea. Originally a rural parish, West Ham was the last stop before entering London and the first staging post from London. Its proximity to the Capital was key to the area's growth. The great Roman road between London and Colchester was diverted through West Ham's component districts in the twelfth century when Bow Bridge was built. The River Lea was the stimulus for further early industrial activity such as silk-weaving and calico printing. Additionally, but not highly publicised, the distillery trade and production of gunpowder were big business.

The rest of the parish comprised of a scattering of small agricultural hamlets including; Plaistow, Church Lane, Forest Gate (the forest being the then extensive Epping Forest), and Upton. The marshland to the south of the parish was used for grazing cattle and pasturing horses. Places like Upton and Plaistow acted as pleasant rural retreats, attracting big City merchants, who built substantial houses there.

However, the inexorable growth of London had a profound effect on the whole area, particularly after 1844 when legislation restricted many toxic and noxious industries from operating, not only in the capital itself but also westwards, including Middlesex. This resulted in many of these unwanted industries relocating eastwards across the Essex border, spreading along the Thames-side area of West Ham and up to Stratford.

The banks of the Lea, and soon after the Thames, quickly became lined with factories, rendering down animal carcases for tallow, soap and glue and chemical plants producing acids, pharmaceuticals and a vast range of other poisonous products that were considered too obnoxious to manufacture nearer the capital.

In short, the East End had, by the time grandfather arrived, become the dustbin of industry and scant attention was paid to its effect on the local inhabitants and their environment. It was often said that West London had its 'swells' and East London its 'smells'.

The area of the docks into which grandfather disembarked had begun development in the early 1800s primarily with shipbuilding, notably the Ditchburn & Mare Shipbuilding Co. of 1837, later to become the Thames Ironworks & Shipbuilding Company (which in 1900 spawned West Ham United FC – more commonly known as the 'Irons' or 'Hammers') before in 1855 seeing the opening of the Victoria Dock and then the Royal Albert Dock in 1880 (with the King George V Dock following much later in 1921). Then the railway arrived and spurred on further growth of West Ham's industrial capability. The dreary Thames-side marshes were transformed into a huge manufacturing and engineering complex which rivalled the great northern cities.

Knowing nothing of this history my grandfather hoped there might be someone nearby who would be glad of a bob or two, to put him up for a while, whilst he looked for a job. As he walked through the streets he pondered the wisdom of his last decision to disembark in London. He recalled that December night, well over a couple of years ago, when he fled from home, from Mr Massie, his family and the fire and, as he rattled the few coins that he possessed, he reassured himself that life, even in these London slums, would be better than a life in Massie's Bakery.

After half-an-hour of walking through closely packed streets, brightened only by streams of brown stained sunshine that leaked through the alleys, he felt a little weary.

Little did grandfather know it, but he had arrived in Canning Town where settlement began on the low-lying marshland fronting the Thames around the early 1840s. The introduction of the railway into the area, Mare's Ship-building Works in 1846, the Victoria dock in 1855 and a number of chemical industries, created a demand for housing so two new towns within what was once the rural parish of West Ham, 'Canning Town' and 'Hallsville' were established to accommodate the influx of workers and their families. Unfortunately the rapid and uncontrolled development that took place lacked a proper water supply and sewage disposal and many locals succumbed to deadly diseases, such as smallpox and cholera.

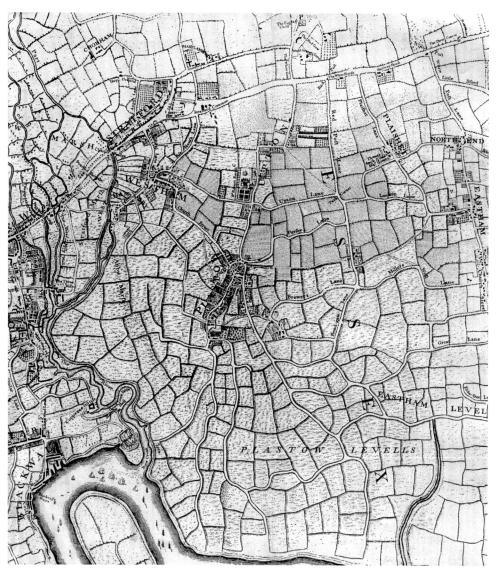

West Ham and Surrounding District in the early eighteenth century. Note: Stratford Common, West Ham Abbey, Woodgrange Farm, Ass House Lane (Vicarage Lane), Upton Lane (Plashet Road) and Stratford Lane (West Ham Lane). Also the absence of Barking Road and Railways making for what must have been a very rural, if somewhat featureless, landscape.

West Ham circa 1880. Note: Large tracts of land striil not built upon, West Ham and Plaistow Marshes, West Ham Park, the absence of the Royal Albert and King George V Docks and the appearance of Barking Road and Railways. By this time Canning Town has appeared almost at the mouth of the River Lee and two of London's lanmark dock had appeared, Victoria and (?). Still a largely rural landscape once much of the area though the ominous creep of urban development is clearly visible from the west.

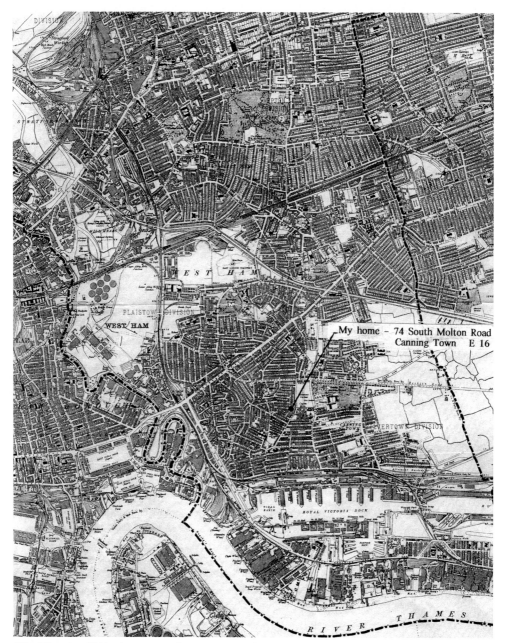

My home – 74 South Molton Road
Canning Town   E 16

*West Ham circa 1940. A vast maze of streets, new Dock approaches – Silvertown Way, Beckton Bypass,
and the Royal Docks complete. In a little over 100 years the whole landscape has altered becoming a vast and
untidy urban sprawl and little by way of open tracks.*

By the time of his arrival in the late 1880s, the separate hamlets of Plaistow, Stratford, Upton, Forest Gate and Canning Town had merged into a sea of bricks and West Ham had become the eighth largest town in Britain attracting workers from all over the country to work in its factories, the docks and the Beckton Gas Works. In 1886 it was accorded the status of a Municipal Borough and three years later became a County Borough, growing much later (1921) to some 300,000. Ships from foreign ports around the world passed through the East End's docks and many seamen came and stayed ashore just as grandfather did.

Grandfather turned into Granville Road in Canning Town and could think of nothing else but the need to bed down somewhere, even if it was only for the night. In every street he passed he had seen children playing street games whilst their parents chatted in doorways or sat on window sills, relaxing in the last hours of sunshine. This road seemed a happy one and he paused for a moment to watch the children play, shout and skip. My grandfather's mood began to lighten, the nightmare of the ship already starting to hurt less. With Massie's fire still burning in his mind, it seemed that the East End of London was awaiting him with open arms.

My grandfather's progress down Granville Road was partially obstructed by a group of children of varying ages and sizes, waiting in turn to dance a one-step in and out of a large skipping rope that spanned the road from kerb to kerb. He went towards one of the taller girls who was waiting to take her turn at the rope end and asked her where he could get some 'digs' for the night. The teenager, startled by grandfather's unfamiliar accent, took fright and ran to a man in his early twenties, sitting on the window sill of No. 72, smoking a pipe. My grandfather clearly heard her Cockney tones as she explained to the young man, 'That man over there talks funny and wants to dig something'. This, 'talking funny' was understandable as my grandfather, even relating his story to me some forty years later, still retained his unmistakeable Liverpudlian accent.

The man called grandfather over and introduced himself as Josiah Hadley, a local dockworker. An almost instant rapport developed as, like my grandfather, he too had been on a sea trip to Australia some two years earlier. Josiah was the elder brother of Kate-Clara, the skipping teenager who had been so troubled by grandfather's unfamiliar accent. The two men immediately struck up a friendship as they sat on a windowsill, reminiscing and comparing sea stories.

Grandfather told Josiah of his plight and meagre wealth and was soon taken indoors to meet Josiah's mother, Mrs Amelia Hadley. He was given a cup of tea and an offer to stay there overnight. And stay he did – for the next four years. He never did return to live in Bootle.

The Hadleys were a large and fairly poor family but they opened up their humble home to the stranger, despite the overcrowding that this unexpected arrival caused them. The very next day Josiah (known affectionately as 'Sigh') took my grandfather back to the docks in the hope of finding him a job there, for despite the many factories in the area, work was not always easy to come by for thousands were flocking into the area, often with only harsh living conditions their scant reward for striving for a better life. The employment position was worsened by the influx of foreign immigrants, mainly from Germany, Italy, and Ireland. All of those who did manage to find work and a place to live were forced to accept rapidly worsening conditions.

Work was mainly casual, as well as seasonal, so people could only afford to live in overcrowded, inadequate housing, which lacked even the basic amenities. Adding to this, pollution, unhealthy working conditions, and long hours, meant accidents and deaths were an everyday occurrence.

Chimneys on houses and factories would constantly pour out black, sulphurous smoke and the inefficiency of burning whatever fuel was readily and economically available, like wood or coal, ensured that much of the un-burnt carbon would fall out in the form of soot and grit. It blackened the fabric of the houses and other buildings and further added to the drabness of the dingy terraces in the labyrinth of back streets. Women fought a constant battle to keep their homes soot-free and their washing as white as possible. The amount of particulate matter in the air was never more apparent than in the winter, when snow fell and the black flecks peppered its surface. Houses rarely had their windows open, their residents preferring to keep the heat and smell indoors and the industrial grime out.

Some of the more up-market houses had window shutters hinged against their walls and foot-scrapers to clean their boots from the filth of the street. High up on the walls of some terraces were Fire Insurance Shields to mark them out as being insured against fire. These were instantly identified by the firemen of the day when such early fire-services were often private. Had my grandfather and his family had the opportunity to obtain a Fire Insurance Shield their situation might have turned out somewhat different.

With Josiah Hadley's help my grandfather was in luck that day and he was offered a position as a labourer in the Royal Albert Dock. His reliability and hard work soon paid off and he was promoted to Ganger, and then a crane driver for 'Spillers' – a large flour millers – where he worked for over thirty-five years.

In those early years of his transition to the East End life, John Maudesley began courting the eldest Hadley daughter, Eva, but her domineering ways and her attempts to curb grandfather's natural free spirit took their toll on him and he grew increasingly closer to her younger sister; the very girl who had fled from him on his first day in the neighbourhood.

Kate-Clara and my grandfather married locally in December 1898 when he was twenty-four and she was twenty. In their first twenty-two years of marriage, my grandparents brought eleven new faces into the world. Life

John Maudesley in his wedding year, circa 1898.

was hard and money scarce as my grandmother fought to raise her ever-increasing family. To supplement the family income, she took in laundry and pressing work, using old cast-iron flats off the kitchen grate. Her main line of business came from the white linen coffin shrouds, used by the under-takers in the Aldgate and Whitechapel area.

Matters were made worse when my grandmother's own mother, Amelia sadly passed away, thereby causing her elder sister Eva (unmarried and still smarting from my grandfather's rejecting her) to leave the Hadley family home in Granville Road and seek refuge with Kate-Clara and John, who were then living in nearby Clarkson Street. This 'temporary arrangement' lasted for twenty-eight years and was a major source of domestic conflict. It often caused my grandfather to threaten to go back to sea as he deemed this 'the lesser of two evils'.

My mother, Ellen, was born in 1905 to John and Kate Maudesley, the fourth of the eventually eleven children my grandmother bore.

Although thankfully managing to escape the worst ravages of the Great War, which affected so many working class families in the East End of London and throughout 'Great Britain', the Maudesley family were not without tragedy, suffering the premature deaths of five of their 11 offspring: John (aged 2) developed pneumonia through mastoids; Kate (aged 6) contracted meningitis following a fall down the stairs; Walter (aged 3) also died from pneumonia after measles; and later Jessie (aged 17) was killed by a lorry in Christmas week 1935; and Frank (aged 26) drowned at a holiday camp on what was to be his last 'bachelor' holiday. Such was the harshness of life in the East End of London.

CHAPTER FOUR

Between the Wars – Another Unplanned Arrival in the East End

I was born almost exactly between the end of the First World War and the start of the Second World War. I made my way into the world just five months past wedlock. One can only imagine the furore caused within my maternal grandparents' orderly and moral home. I, who unknowingly was responsible for causing alarm and disgust in the final year of the roaring 1920s, was expected to make my first public appearance in late August. It would kick-start urgent wedding plans to avoid my inheriting any stigma attached to the offspring of unmarried parents. I made my debut some 36 hours after that of my cousin Joyce Galvin, the second daughter of my mother's eldest sister, in the very next bed of the Maternity Ward at Howard's Road Hospital in Plaistow, on 28th August 1929.

My parents came respectively from a large and not so large family, with mum having ten brothers and sisters, whilst dad had four. The reason for the Smiths falling below the then-average six children hinged upon the fact that my paternal grandmother, Emma, died at an early age, shortly after giving birth to a daughter, Dorothy, and this after her husband (my unknown paternal grandfather) had 'buggered off!', though not with another woman, as might be advanced for a marriage break-up of today, but through his wife's spendthrift habit and over-generosity to all who realised her weakness.

With work hard to come by and money very tight, my dad's father couldn't keep pace with his wife's 'easy-come, easy-go' philanthropy, deciding that enough was enough and disappearing without trace. Whether it was his desertion or her post-natal depression which contributed to, or caused, Emma's early death, is not known. But it meant the fatherless Smiths (except Dorothy) were put in the care of Dr Barnardo's Home for Orphans in Stepney, and later at Brentwood, until they each reached working age (at just fourteen!), when they were taken in by their grandmother Mrs Bridges and Aunt Maud successively.

I don't know if my mother was kicked out for bringing shame on the family, or whether she was allowed to stay at my grandparent's house until such time as my existence could no longer be disguised. Perhaps my actual arrival was when my mother finally chose, or was forced, to leave the family home at No. 23. Whichever one of the foregoing situations my dear mum

1929 – Cousin Joyce Galvin (left) and Charles Smith (right) aged three months.

found herself in, without support from my father who was sailing round Africa in the Union Castle passenger ship Gloucester Castle, I was never told. I remain completely unaware of how I came to be brought up in the house that was to be my home for the next twenty-five years.

In her desperation my mother found a single room to let in the same road as my grandparents and their eldest married daughter, my Aunt Floss. The move up the road, whenever it took place, was to the home of the Moss family, comprising an elderly father and his partially handicapped son, Ernie. He must have been about twenty years older than my mother. Though themselves rented the house, they sub-let the upstairs front room for a shilling per week (approximately 5p) leaving them to pay just half-a-crown per week (approximately 12½p) for the rest of the house.

Mr Moss died when I was about four years old and his son Ernie allowed us to use the tiny third bedroom for me to sleep in when my father was ashore. Ernie must have been in his mid-to-late forties, a simple soul who had not had an easy life with his domineering old father. He was a bachelor with a pockmarked face, resulting from smallpox in his twenties. His clothes were shabby and his hygiene left much to be desired, but all his faults didn't stop me from loving him because he was always there for me. He had an unusual taste in decorating that he would exercise whenever a new idea came to mind. Once, he fixed several papier-mâché egg trays, coloured in black and white check around the fireplace. I didn't have the heart to tell him about how dangerous *that* could be. On another occasion, he sawed the kitchen door in half to make a gate for his chicken run. Not that he dearly loved the chickens; he and his father used to bring them in . . . just in time for Christmas!

As my mother worked, Ernie Moss looked after me when I wasn't with my grandmother. This was a wonderful arrangement for me to be shielded from parental and grandparental discipline, and Ernie doted on me. He would often take me to and from school, treat me to cold custard in a brown glazed earthenware dish (to this day I still prefer cold thick custard) or sometimes, when I was lucky, he would give me a large enamel bowl full of silver sand for me to play with; sand which he had stolen from Fox's yard before it was hauled in large carts to the Canning Town Glassworks.

Ernie died when I was about seven and my mother took over the tenancy. The prized possessions and fixtures inside our, and most other local homes, were a black-leaded grate/oven, a gas wash-boiler, a butler sink and the pièce de résistance, which set a family apart from its neighbours: an upright piano, although no one in our house could play it! The house fronted directly onto the pavement within a closely packed maze of back streets. On the corners of many of these dingy streets there was often an equally dingy shop of some sort, each of them trying desperately to eke out a meagre living. The irony of the locals' plight was that many of the streets were grandly named after places that most had never heard or even dreamed of – somewhere in that far off unknown area of West England, South Molton, Totnes, Charford, Exeter or Brent. Gardens were virtually non-existent as each house had its own backyard, the enclosed area of which was probably about 20 square yards; not enough room to swing a cat in.

My Grandfather and I

From the time we spent together, I was able to form a first hand impression of both sides of his personality, like his humour and his devotion to his family, against his stubbornness, his jealous streak, his quickness to take offence and his intolerance of even the slightest hint of effeminacy in a man.

The light-hearted theme which I hope you will find accompanies my personal recollections, will hopefully bear testament to my inheriting some of my grandfather's sense of humour. A humour which was spontaneous, often cutting, but the type traditionally associated with the North West, especially the Liverpuddlians who made light of their day-to-day problems by joking, rather than moaning, about their plight. I too have learned the value of laughter in times of worry and unhappiness and, like my grandfather, always tried to look on the bright side of life.

Although not rich, he was as generous as he could be with such a large family and detested meanness in others, highlighting this characteristic with such comments as, 'She's so bleedin' mean she rolls up the pavement at night and takes it indoors.' Although I still remember some of his many quips and philosophies, they are too numerous to record and perhaps hold your attention, so suffice it for me to record just some examples, viz: Women whose name he couldn't remember were known as 'Fanny Fernackerpan' or 'Nitty Nora' whilst most strange men were called 'Bacon Bonce' and, if you asked him what so-and-so did for a living, he would likely reply, 'He's a masticator! He chews bread for our ducks!'. About 'posing' neighbours, he would make a comment like, 'She's got fruit on her sideboard and she's got no one in hospital!'.

One Maudesley characteristic which I have often been accused of harbouring is that of stubbornness. Like my grandfather, if I don't want to do something then the 'John Maudesley' within me pumps up the adrenaline and downloads the stubborn factor to my heels, ensuring they stay firmly planted in the ground awaiting that irresistible force to arrive to overcome my stubborn immovability.

I am thankful, however, not to have been a legatee of his obvious jealous streak, which my grandfather openly, and unjustly, directed at my grandmother. This can be illustrated by his quizzing me whenever my grandmother took me out, mostly to the pictures, about who she sat next to and did she speak to any men and who spoke first?, etc. I never did find out if I accompanied my grandmother on local trips, or to Southend and Margate, for company or as an informer. Though it was quite common to let the 'Rent Man', the 'Pru Man' (insurance salesman) and the 'Tally Man' (loan shark) into one's house, grandfather forbade any such familiarity and all male callers were kept 'on the doorstep' – 'Where they belong!'

My grandfather was also quick to take offence, though not in an aggressive way, but rather a sulky-like 'don't talk to me' way. His fierce pride (almost as destructive an emotion as his jealousy) made it impossible for him to be readily forgiving, leaving the 'offender' to apologise first or make reparations. Those who didn't remained permanently on the 'persona non grata' list. During the German Blitz on London, I once refused his order to get into the air-raid shelter and told him, 'It's my life not yours!', whereupon he stalked off into the house and remained there despite the bombardment from above and the pleas from both my grandmother and mother to take cover. About a week later, when my pride proved inferior to his, I apologised, and only then was I allowed to resume our relationship. This reconciliation was eased by his needing his monthly haircut which I had been giving him for a couple of years. The coiffure was simplicity itself as I wielded the hand clippers in an all-over haircut that was only about ⅛" away from total baldness.

I am not sure how my grandfather would have reacted in today's sexually liberated times, where gender-bending, gays and lesbians are part of everyday life. His intolerance of 'cissies' or 'nancy boys' was probably due to his bad experiences as a young man on a maiden sea voyage. Of his four surviving sons who had reached adulthood, the three eldest – John, Alf and Frank – were (in grandfather's eyes) real men with man's jobs but, unfortunately the youngest, Stanley, was a quieter and more genteel person than his brothers and below the macho standard required from their father. Relations between grandfather and Stanley deteriorated to the farcical situation where he completely ignored his youngest son throughout the remainder of his life, and this despite Stanley never marrying, but devoting himself to being the bread-winner and carer, as both his parents became aged and increasingly more reliant upon him for their support. My grandfather would never refer to Stanley by name, but refer to him as the 'queer fella'. Whilst idolising my grandfather, I also had the greatest respect for Stanley's fortitude in the difficult and almost untenable circumstances which prevailed in the Maudesley home from the time of his demobilisation from the wartime forces in 1946, until the death of my grandfather in 1962. Only Stanley knows if the insults and humiliation heaped upon him were justified.

A lasting image

For all the time that I knew him, my grandfather had no teeth and refused to have false ones fitted, yet it suited him and I was never aware of his dental deficiency. All I remember was his ability to constantly amuse me with his facial contortions where his chin could almost touch his nose and he did a fair take-off of the popular cartoon character of the day – Popeye! My grand-mother would often buy a pig's trotter for him and boil it until it was tender and edible. This meal (as well as the evil-smelling salt fish) seemed to form his staple diet, eaten at any time of the day, often taking him an hour or more to dispose of it little by little with the aid of a small, sharp knife. I would stand at his side with my elbows on the table supporting my chin, watching him, in absolute fascination at the movement of his toothless lower jaw chewing the small pieces of meat over and over again.

The East End Docklands area of my childhood, which encompassed the Royal Docks from North Woolwich, Silvertown, Custom House, Canning Town and Poplar, was still trying to come to terms with the legacy left from the 1926 General Strike, of unemployment and associated poverty. Work was scarce and wages were low as the men competed for labouring jobs on a daily hire basis at the dock gates. Some went to sea as deck hands or general dogsbodies. The alternative, if they could afford the fare and conditions, was on the new car assembly production line at Ford's Dagenham Works.

One day grannie's cousin Bill, later in life to be known as 'Lurverly bitta duff Nell' Hadley (duff being Bill's term for boiled suet pudding – a main element of our diet), was home from his sea-going job and popped in to see grandad and grannie. Reflecting the poor state of the economy, he was like many men of the time, wearing borrowed trousers that were too short for him. His 'short' trousers revealed an anaemic white leg above the top of his working boots. Grandad sarcastically said 'Hey Bill are they short long-uns or long short-uns?' Bill looked embarrassed by his disheveled look and before he could think what to say in response, grandad added with a wry smile, 'Why don't yer put some bread and jam on yer boots and invite yer trousers down for tea!'. We all had a good laugh at that, a typical East End reaction to deprivation.

It says a lot for men of those times whom, however poor and consequently desperate they were, never resorted to robbing their own kind, either within or outside their homes. Money and material possessions were gained by working. Almost all the surrounding families were 'in the same boat' as each other so they had very little, or nothing, to be robbed of. However, companies and employers were fair game.

Charlie Barker was my dad's cousin, and he was the family's 'lovable rogue'. He smuggled and 'nicked' everything to order. As a result he was well known to the local constabulary and was raided by suspicious officers many a time. He was mystifyingly always found to be 'clean'. Charlie hid all his ill-gotten gains down a very deep manhole in his back garden, disguising the cast iron cover plate with a washing mangle placed strategically over it. If stolen goods couldn't fit into the manhole he was smart enough to ensure that whatever had come into his possession was shifted in double quick time without the need to have it hidden in his house. The sewers of the day left much to be desired with rats and disease commonplace. But it didn't seem to stop Charlie's clients demand. In those days of course no questions were asked!

One thing that always amazed me was, despite the absence of today's comparatively generous State Benefits, the adults of the 1930s always seemed to find money for their packet of Woodbines or Players cigarettes, the odd tanner (sixpence) on a horse and a couple of pints of ale every week down the 'local'.

My father neither craved nor aspired to material things, just contentment. He inherited his mother's generosity in that he would have given his last penny away without a moment of hesitation. When my father reached the working age of fourteen, he was sent to work in the Tate & Lyle sugar refinery in Silvertown but his slight frame was not strong enough to sustain the demands of lugging the heavy sacks of sugar. His lack of education condemned him too.

When he turned sixteen the First World War ended, and he thought he would like to see the world and get paid for it whilst, at the same time, becoming independent of his mother's family. A couple of years later he went across the road from the factory into the Victoria and Albert Docks and signed on as a 'sculleryman' on a ship that had docked there. During his life he used his meagre seagoing wages to ensure my mother, sister and I never went hungry and the rent was always paid on time. When he died, he owned nothing more than the clothing on his back and a few bits in the wardrobe where he secreted his supply of Teachers whisky. But he was never in debt, owing nobody a penny.

Like most men of the time, my father did enjoy betting on the horses. Before betting became organised and regulated, illegal 'street betting' was common-place in the East End of my youth. Some of our neighbours acted as 'bookies runners' taking the bets of the locals to hand over to an unknown 'Mr Big' for a small commission. Sixpence was about the most that people could afford to wager in those days. Of course the only ones to profit were the bookies. I recall hearing from one of our neighbours of the time that 'the ruination of the working class was fast women and slow horses!'

I am not sure if my mother's penchant for organising everything domestically and financially was a natural gift or whether it was heaped upon her by my father's abdication of all home responsibilities in his pursuit of a carefree life. Being one of the eldest in the large Maudesley family, my mother and her eldest sister Eva, had to do their share of helping out around the house, including looking after their seven siblings. Mother was considered average in educational achievements but subsequently displayed her talents not only for neat and legible handwriting, but also for arithmetic – a talent which was to stand her in good stead when she entered the rag trade on a part-time basis, buying and selling to supplement my dad's wages. Mum had always worked. From around the age of sixteen she worked as a housemaid/nursemaid to the Waller family (Custom House's premier butcher) at their large Dagenham house. Later she worked as a waitress for Mecca Cafes, serving the upper class and showbiz celebrities including Ivor Novello, Noel Coward, and Marie Lloyd. During the 1920s it was the place to be!

In her days as a waitress, she was told of the daily increasing affluence of businesses in the East End's Aldgate and Whitechapel areas. She decided to tap into this rich source by dealing at warehouses in Houndsditch. The main 'sell everything' warehouse was 'Deyongs', where she managed to persuade them to sell her goods at trade price and then retailed them at a modest profit. Eventually others took her goods into the many local offices and factories, so setting up a thriving agency. Her success was in adopting the Roman Latin 'SPQR' (the abbreviation for 'Senatus Populusque Romanus'). But to my mother, the initials 'SPQR' stood for, 'Small Profits Quick Returns'.

The Deyongs warehouse adopted a trade price code system, used to deter non bona-fide traders from knowing the wholesale price. I learned off by heart the code word – 'BUCKINGHAM'. The name Buckingham, comprising ten different letters, was used to represent numbers 1 to 10. So an item costing 19s 6d would be tagged 'BA/N', whilst something costing £6 15s 3d (an absolute fortune in those days,) would have a price tag showing 'N/BI/C'. My mother used this code on my dad whenever he had the temerity to ask 'How much did you pay for that?' Her reply completely baffled him – 'BA'! As far as I knew, he didn't crack it until he was about 'KA'!

Although completely opposite to my father, my mother kept the marriage ticking over by 'allowing' dad to indulge in his carefree life so long as she could 'do her own thing' without criticism or interruption. They may have been reasonably poor in the early thirties, living in one room with a drawer from my gran's chest of drawers as a cot for my sister and I, but thereafter were always there for me as the best parents I could have had.

Dad spent most of his working and my early life at sea. With each round trip lasting about four months and home leave of about twelve days between trips, I didn't see a lot of him. What with mum going from success to success in her selling business and dad away at sea, I almost knew what it must have felt like for him as an orphan, if it were not for my grandparents.

CHAPTER FIVE

Between the Wars – Life in the East End

Between the Wars, the people of Canning Town were united in a common bond, helping each other out during the hard times. Much of their leisure time was spent together, visiting a pub, dance hall, boxing or a football match, whilst an outing to Epping Forest, Southend or a working holiday hop-picking in Kent was something to look forward to.

Almost all the housing was rented and the landlords of such properties were openly opposed to carrying out essential repairs to the homes that were often devoid of even the basic amenities. Many houses were shared between different families on an 'up and down' basis, using a common front door and WC.

In the 1930s, the Borough Council sought to alleviate some of the worst aspects of housing and poverty with a programme of slum clearance and health promotion. Hundreds of Victorian houses were condemned as 'unfit for human habitation' and were demolished. New houses with modern facilities were built and new services including clinics, nurseries and a lido were opened. The long delays previously faced by the traffic into and out of the area, were reduced by the construction of new approach roads and the Silvertown Way. This cut a swathe through the former slums and provided a 'Road to the Empire', bypassing the bottleneck at Tidal Basin.

The combination of heavy industry and poor social conditions, created by inadequate housing and public services, stimulated much 'left-wing' activity and eventually the mix of poverty and cultural diversity encouraged the proliferation of religious and social welfare within the community, which was often supported by wealthy outside patrons, like today's United Nations Relief for poor and undeveloped countries.

In an effort to improve their working and living conditions, the workers sought the solidarity of Trade Unions and political activities to further their cause. Canning Town became the focus of a number of new movements and several of the people involved, including Keir Hardie, became leading lights in the emerging Labour Party.

It was against this backdrop that my early East End childhood was a curious blend of naiveté and craft; an environment where one was expected to be seen but not heard. In the harsh practical way of the poorer working class, one was a child yet not a child; loved yet feeling unloved. Another home rule was to always respect one's elders, which included being nice to all such persons, particularly visitors to the house, even if one disliked them. I painfully and embarrassingly remember being literally swept up by aunts and other female friends of the family, to be enfolded in large arms and hoisted off my feet into a vice-like embrace from which there was no escape. Whilst my breathing was being restricted to the point of suffocation, the lower half of my small body was increasingly pulled into the unyielding whalebone stiffeners of a corset. Eventually I would be released, breathless and squeezed like a tube of toothpaste, hearing the inevitable exclamation of, 'Doesn't he look like his father!'

My first home holds many vivid memories for me. The one room, which I shared with my mother, had been the Moss's main bedroom up until the time that Mrs Moss died. The father and son then used the other two bedrooms, as well as the downstairs rooms, scullery and outside toilet. This meant that we had no cooking or toilet facilities, though we had an open fire grate supplemented by a Valour paraffin-oil stove on which a kettle could be perched. Our toilet merely consisted of a chamber pot. For eating we crossed the road to grandmother's house, where we'd spend most of the day.

There, grandad's favourite targets were 'posing' neighbours. He would rattle off a succession of caustic and often humourous comments. His particular favourite however, was 'I knew them when they didn't have a pot to piss in' adding after a short pause, 'Or a bleedin' window to throw it out of!' A reflection of sanitation in those times.

With my father away at sea and my mother out working to make 'ends meet', I spent considerable time in my grandparents house in South Molton Road. As was the custom of the day, the house was always open to visitors, with family and friends regularly popping in for a 'cuppa'. When visitors came to houses in those times, probably in the absence of TV's as distractions, they nearly always referred to the children of the house. They made polite conversation, commenting on how much they had grown or referring to their likeness to their parents. On one occasion I recall that one of grannie's friends, looking at me, said, 'Doesn't he look like his dad?' Grandad quick as a flash retorted 'Yes! Yer can tell his mother didn't take in lodgers!' It was only many years later that I understood his reference.

The closeness of the houses and the large blank factory wall that seemed to permanently block out the sunlight made the living room, then known as the kitchen, very dark and gloomy. There were times when the odd ray of summer sunshine filtered through the narrow gap between the houses and the factory and then on through the heavy lace curtains. On these rare occasions the sunbeam would split into a myriad coloured lights as it passed through our ornamental glass centrepiece – the coveted 'epergne' status symbol.

The decor of our house, if one could call it that, usually consisted of painted walls with a picture rail, a dado rail to protect the wall from chair backs, high moulded skirting and a whitewashed ceiling. Later a craze emerged to panel the walls using two patterns of wallpaper whilst on plainly painted walls a piece of sponge was dipped into different coloured paints and stippled over the surface. It seemed to me that paint came in just three colours, plus white. Everywhere was painted brown, cream or *eau-de-nil*. Hallways, or passages, were often decorated from the floor to the dado with lincruster; a heavily embossed paper soaked for hours before being applied to the walls with smelly glue and painted with several coats. The top part of the picture rail would be papered with a gaudy, patterned paper. To remove the lincruster was a long hard job as it usually had to be burnt off. Its strength was never more evident than after the German Blitz when walls in bombed houses were literally supported from collapse by the hero lincruster and its many coats of paint.

My grandmother would give me two jobs on most Sunday mornings; one was to rub 2-inch thick triangular blocks of rock salt into fine granules for cooking and sprinkling onto food. The other was to tear old newspapers into squares of about 8 inches, gather them into a straight-sided pile, drive a hole into one corner with a large nail and coal hammer and then thread a piece of string through it to hang at the side of the loo pan or on the back of the door, as 'East End tissues'. Toilet rolls were for the rich so we had to make do with newspaper from which the printing ink oh too easily transferred itself to one's backside!

All local houses had outside toilets. These would be about 30 inches square on the floor with a high, rusty, cast-iron cistern. A WC pan would be set into a base of concrete, surmounted by a wall-to-wall bench seat made from floor-boards and joined together with a hole cut into it. Along the front edge would be a 4 or 5 inch board to prevent the seat edge cutting into the legs. Naturally, over time the boards shrank and their grain became proud. As a result, they did not encourage lengthy 'sittings'. If you did stay too long, then you would emerge with a large ring mark on your backside known colloquially as the 'shitter's ring'!

There was no window and often no light, except from the large gaps deliberately left at both the top and bottom of the board door. As a result, it was always an icy cold, dark, dank place, even in summer. This extension to the house was politely known as a 'carsey'.

The outside toilets were in the main responsible for countless soiled beds – especially in winter. Some people were simply too afraid of the dark to con-template a spooky trip to the 'carsey' at night and so chamber pots or 'Po's' were commonplace. Often being filled to the brim each morning, they required careful handling down the stairs before being tipped gingerly down the kitchen sink! The journey to the outside toilet was all too hazardous. In consequence many houses reeked of pee as one entered the passage, nowadays called the hall, causing sarcastic remarks like 'Mrs So-&-So has dropped the

Top (Bidder Street) and Bottom (Swanscombe Street): Typical 'Old Canning Town' pre-war working-class housing. Note the boot scrapers adjacent to the front doors and the window shutters. Such living conditions amid an impoverished environment would, today qualify for Third World aid with their inadequate heating, minimum regard to hygiene and very basic toilet facilities, with a tin bath in the kitchen and an outside lavatory often shared with many adults and children alike, sometimes by more than one or two families.

piss-pot again!' However, if she had successfully negotiated the routine early morning trip to the outside toilet she would be elevated to the sarcastic title of 'Piss-pot jerker!'

Of course being outside, damp, dark and musty places, the outside toilet was always a natural hiding place for all kinds of creepy-crawlies, mice and the occasional rat! The gap between seat and concrete plinth was a favourite place to hide! One day when I was about 12 years old, grannie Maudsley was 'on the throne' with her passion-killer drawers around her ankles when a large rat courageously poked its head out between her legs. She let out a hor-rendous scream of absolute fear causing grandad and I to run out to see what had happened. Luckily, doors for the outside toilets had a gap of about 6 inches top and bottom, supposedly for ventilation. The terrified rat ran out under the door and headed straight for an old chest of drawers kept in the back yard where grandad kept his 'odds-and-sods'. The frightened rat dived underneath the chest of drawers to hide. Quick as a shot, grandad lifted it up but quickly dropped it as the rat jumped to take flight. The chest of drawers just nipped the rat and sent it scurrying for the nearby drain-pipe from the toilet roof gutter. Grandad told me to watch at the bottom arming me with a 'copper' stick while he ran inside to boil a kettle to pour down the pipe. That did the trick and by the time grandad got down off the toilet roof the rat barely managed to stagger out. Grandad hit the rat with the coal hammer kept nearby to break up large chunks of coal in those days and then slung it over next-door's garden – he never liked them anyway! When he cleaned out under the toilet seat he found that the rat had set up home under the 'shitter'. There were potatoes and scraps that had been thrown out for the birds and loads of chewed-up newspaper, the remains of our carefully prepared 'East End tissues'! After that scare, grannie always raked underneath the toilet seat on each trip with the 'copper' stick, making quite sure that 'Roland' didn't leave any family to jump up between her lillywhite, varicose veined legs again. Actually I was never quite sure who would have been the most terrified in the event of any future encounters!

One day my mother was looking to make some improvements in our lives. She decided that the drab outside toilet needed brightening up. She had gotten hold of an old tin of maroon paint. The only place she could think to use it was on the old, 'bum' worn wooden platform that served as our toilet seat. Unfor-tunately, on coming home from school at lunch time, I had decided that I needed to use the toilet before lunch. I made straight for the outside toilet. Taking down my school boy shorts and underpants, I immediately plonked my backside firmly upon the platform. Imagine my surprise, having done my 'business' when I attempted to lift off. My puny white little bum was now firmly attached to the freshly painted wooden platform! Using my hands to attempt to prise myself up and away from my potentially lengthy incarcera-tion in the family 'carsey' just seemed to make matters worse as my hands also became covered in this sticky maroon paint! Mum was deaf to my screams of horror until when she came to look where I was, she heard my shouts of desperation from the outside toilet. She was never a patient or understanding woman at the best of times and despite my tears, harangued me with a passion, calling me all the 'silly little sods that there ever was' or words to that effect. With little sympathy for my screams, which was usually a bad sign as it was associated with the removal of strong sticking plaster being ripped off my constantly grazed knees, we eventually managed between us to achieve 'lift-off'. This was immediately followed by a thorough 'slagging off' which was no less painful. All thoughts of lunch were immediately forgotten as margarine and parrafin was liberally and roughly applied to remove the maroon 'shitters ring' I was now wearing. I was in such a state both physically and mentally, that I was kept home for the rest of the afternoon. If a match had been struck any where near to me that afternoon, then I would have gone into orbit around Canning Town and probably be fined for low flying. For the first time that I can remember, I would have gladly opted for an afternoon at school. The carsey toilet seat eventually took all of three days to dry; after a further repainting to hide up the bare 'bum' patches I had caused.

Family bath-times were usually restricted to a Friday, or sometimes a Saturday, for a once weekly, all over soak, including one's hair. I recall one particular press advert for a shampoo called 'AMAMI' which declared proudly, 'Friday night is Amami night!' Our oval shaped bath was made of galvanised steel of about 3 feet long by 2 feet wide and 20 inches deep. It had a handle at each end for transporting it in and out of the house and for hanging it on the fence during the rest of the week. In winter it would sit in the kitchen in front of the open fire or the oven with its black-leaded polish and adjacent firebox. This meant one side of the bath and consequently, one side of one's body would get considerably warmer than the other. The bath's dimensions dictated a 'knees up under the chin' posture for anybody over 4 feet tall, so adults had to stand upright to ensure the cleansing of the lower body. If an adult *did* decide to sit down to soak, there was always the risk of large hips becoming stuck fast within the bath's restricted confines. The alternative, for those families that could afford it, was a bungalow bath, about 5 feet long with straight sides and rounded ends which did allow a degree of sitting and soaking.

A more convenient location for the bath was in the scullery, housing the coal/wood-fired copper for boiling wash-water. In the adjacent corner was a four inches deep, brown, earthenware sink, supplied by the only tap in the house. At the end of a length of ugly lead piping, it seemed only capable of delivering ice-cold water and, like the outside WC, had to be thawed out each winter. The bath was kept warm using firewood, as coal was too expensive. The local children, me included, scrounged firewood from local shops and the nearby 'Loders and Nucolene' margarine factory in Silvertown. One day whilst I was out with my uncle Alf looking for firewood, he persuaded me to go into Woodcock's, the local undertakers. Naively, I asked the old man in the shop, as Alf instructed, if he had any empty boxes! Grumpy old Woodcock wasn't amused. I ran out of the shop sure that if he managed to grab me then, I would have been in one of those large polished boxes myself.

The pecking order on Friday nights was youngest first; dads last. We used mostly the same water that was continually ladled out and topped up from an occasional hot kettle or saucepan. By the end of this bathing ritual, the bath was far too heavy to be moved to the outside drain or tipped on to the concrete yard, so buckets and saucepans were used to ladle out the water until it could be manually lifted out. Often, in more crowded accomodation, the waste water was simply thrown out of the window, regardless of whether it was at the front of the property or if anyone was passing by. We had the carbolic type or coal tar brands of soap, like 'Family Health', 'Lifebuoy', and 'Wrights', all of which had strong smells, which as my mother told me, germs couldn't stand. Occasionally, especially if the nit nurse was due to visit school, hair would be washed with 'Derbac' soap, an evil smelling, eye stinging black bar that controlled head lice. This would be followed by the torturous scrapes of a small-toothed comb, used in a most vigorous fashion, for the hunting out of any surviving lice and scurf. It always ended with me crying out desperately for my mum to stop.

Family wash day for the clothes was always a Monday. The whites were the priority and all of them had to be boiled for hours, with 'Sylvan' soap flakes and soda as the only additives. Many local people did not have the luxury of a gas boiler and had to rely on the old fashioned copper, which, in our pre-war house, was a 3 feet block of concrete with a hole in its top and a fire underneath. The bowl of the copper was a large cast-iron cupola about 2 feet in diameter. The grate below, with its small opening, made it almost impossible to throw coal in and so we relied mainly on firewood. To get the boil started it had to be lit at around 6.00 am with wood, collected from Loders & Nucolene or local grocery shops. When broken up, the Loders' oil-impregnated wood burned beautifully. To earn a ha'penny or the princely sum of a whole penny I would cut and chop firewood into regulation length and thickness (9 in × 1 in) to fit the copper's tiny grate. I usually managed to find some from Bradley's Grocery Shop and Sawyers Fish Shop in Fife Road.

To bring the whites to the required, pre-boil state, the dirty linen would be subjected to a vigorous scrub with a block of washing soap against a ribbed glass washboard and continually dunked in the sink or a bowl of warm water. Once immersed in the copper, the clothes would be pushed down with a copper-stick, fashioned from an old broom handle, which was also used to retrieve the boiled clothes like a fork lifting spaghetti and occasionally for chasing rats! It was then dropped into the family bath for the next stage – mangling.

As the bulk of the mangle, or wringer, with its large wooden rollers and big turning wheel was too heavy and too large for it to fit into the scullery confines, the wringing-out operation was usually carried out in the back yard or in the homemade 'out house'. For efficiency, and to save a high degree of physical effort, two people would operate it; one to feed the washing in and catch it on its way out, the other to turn the large cast-iron wheel that was geared to the wooden rollers. The water from this white wash was wrung out and would then be used to do the family's colours. The damp washing would be hung out to dry on high lines in the tiny back yards after being, 'blued to bring out the whiteness'. Most of the items would then be starched, before ironing.

The poorer families of the East End generally didn't have a 'copper' to boil wash their clothes in. For these and those who couldn't be bothered with washing, which tended to be the majority, there was the 'bagwash'. This consisted of an old, coarse, hessian sack into which all the family's washing, regardless of colour or material was stuffed. As I got older and stronger it was my Monday morning chore to hump the bulging hessian sack down to the 'Diploma Bagwash'. Here it would be ticketed and sealed tight before being thrown, sack 'n all with everyone else's dirty washing into a large tank of boiling water. It was generally returned some 3 or 4 days later more damp than wringing wet, to be put out to dry on the back yard clothes line. Drying clothes outdoors was however always very frustrating. The air was ladened with the soots carried from the local factory chimneys which belched uncontrolled thick dirty smokes continuously. With fierce neighbourly competition between the ladies about the 'whiteness' of the washing, mums were in and out all the time checking on the wind direction. It was amazing what a line of washing could tell about a family's personal hygiene. Back yards always seemed to be full of all kinds of washing, though it was not always freshly hung out as some used the clothes lines as their wardrobe! I remember grandad Maudesley commenting, borne out of his years of observation and dislike of most of the neighbours, about the outdoor ritual of clothes drying 'Her next door can't have any drawers on today 'cos those bloody great green bloomers are out again!'

I hated coming in from school on a damp, cold Monday with the place running with condensation and the smell of washing everywhere. Seeing it draped over fireguards or from lines hastily strung up across the kitchen drove me mad. There was no television to escape to and no dry street to run out and play in, but I would sit, fascinated, by my grandmother ironing those clothes which she had managed to get dry. She would alternately use two old-fashioned flat irons, straight from the hob, onto a very tatty, scorched piece of discarded blanket that had been laid on the kitchen table as an ironing board. My first bit of school handicraft was to make a woven cloth pad for gripping the un-insulated iron handle and I still recall the pride I felt watching my grannie use it for real. With the absence of thermostatically controlled irons, my grandmother would remove the iron from the hob top, turn it upside down and spit on it. If it sizzled and danced across the smooth flat surface and did not evaporate instantly, then the iron was ready.

Because of the cramped and often sparse home conditions, much of the local children's childhood was spent playing in the streets. Kids literally only popped indoors to grab food. And I mean 'grab' as they never wanted to waste time sitting down to eat. This eat-while-you-play food mostly comprised of 'doorsteps' as we didn't have sliced bread in those days. These were constructed out of thick slices of crusty bread liberally smeared with beef dripping, jam but only if it was a weekend, condensed milk, sugar or even HP Sauce if we were lucky enough to get it. In fact almost anything that wouldn't slide off while we played totally oblivious to the horse and dog droppings that littered the back streets. After a day spent outside playing cowboys and Indians, always our favourite, personal cleanliness was forgotten. I would creep indoors usually under cover of darkness and try to avoid mum or grannie Maudesley, to slip into bed without washing. I hated soap and water so much that many a time I would spit-wash my knees before mum saw them in the morning. If she did spot uncleaned limbs she would painfully scrub them with scouring powder as much to teach me a lesson as to get me clean. While she was far from gentle, she did give me absolute freedom to become a typical East End street urchin without ever being sick from my love of grimed-in hands and knees due to my absolute loathing of washing; understandable given it was during the week days always with carbolic soap and cold water!

Food hygiene was minimal with no fridges or freezers. It was kept either in a cupboard or in food-safes protected from fly invasion by perforated metal sides. Flies were always a nuisance because jam, syrup, sugar and condensed milk were kept at the ready by forever being in an uncovered condition, either in an opened tin, jar, packet or, very rarely in a dish. To combat the menace of flies in nearly every household there was the obligatory 'NO!' a leading brand of fly paper hanging from the gas mantle fitting or electric light rose, dangling over the kitchen table. It was essential and relatively effective. Each strip was about 30 inches long covered with a sweet sticky treacle-like 'goo' that attracted the flies more than the ever open tins of condensed milk and jam etc which, because there were no fridges, were constantly left out on the table. Only when the paper was black with flies dead or in some cases still struggling, was a new fly paper put up whilst the other was thrown into the fire. Nothing wasted in those days. I confess to sharing the flies' sweet tooth and secretly dipped my finger into the ever present can of 'Blue Cross' condensed milk at every available opportunity. However, this naughty pastime was stopped when my mother changed the milk from condensed and sticky to evaporated and runny, which could be shaken into tea or on fruit, via two holes in the tin's lid. Its brand name was 'Ideal' and though it was for mum it wasn't for me! It also reduced the flies' attraction to it and therefore left a much more pleasant view at dinnertime.

There were many visitors to my grandparents house in South Molton Road; neighbours, family and friends. But not all were welcome; particularly the mice and the black beetles against whom grandad Maudesley waged a constant war, even making a beer trap to catch the blighters! He'd lay a saucer with a cardboard surround sloping from the floor to its rim, fill it with ale and leave it overnight to attract and ultimately drown the beetles attracted by the beer. Often there were about six or seven dead or just drunk beetles in the saucer every morning. Uncle Alf was terrified of beetles. If he came home late at night he would leap from the front step onto the bottom stair in case one of them got onto his shoes or trousers and he unwittingly carried the insect into bed. When indoors during the day he would always sit with his trousers tucked into his socks. On some nights he would jump into bed with his trousers and metal bike clips on. But I discovered some time later that this was not to stop the beetles crawling up his leg but stop him being late cycling to work after a late night!

I have no recollection of having breakfast cereals out of a packet but I do recall going to school on an early morning diet of real porridge that had been on the boil from around 6.00 am. Sometimes breakfast would be lashings of bread and dripping, plentiful from the Sunday joint, which would last until around mid-week. It was flavoured with the brown or black jelly that nestled in the bottom of the basin. Firstly, one had to break through the cream-coloured dripping fat that had set firmly above it, before arriving at the delicious jelly surprise beneath. I was perhaps more fortunate than many as sometimes my breakfast diet would be alternated with homemade bread pudding, apple tart or even Kemps shortcakes or oval Empress biscuits dunked in hot, sweet tea.

'Squeezing a quart into a pint pot' was a common saying of the day and was used to describe the conditions found in many East End homes. Families grew in their numbers within houses that were never designed to accommodate a family exceeding two adults and three children. Additional strains on over-crowding were caused by aged parents or other relatives who frequently moved into the cramped homes for financial reasons. Sometimes this arrange-ment was reversed as young couples, struggling to raise a family on their low wages, moved in with their parents.

No matter what financial difficulties the husband found himself in, he would rarely allow his wife to go to work leaving the parents-in-law to look after the children. Poverty never overcame pride in the East End.

It was in such conditions that grannie Maudesley raised a family of eleven children, whilst providing board for her elder sister and brother and all in a three bedroom terraced house! How she and all the other mothers coped in solving their family's numerous accommodation problems, not to mention the task of feeding and clothing them, has always intrigued me and I have come to accept that it was a logistical feat unrivalled in today's family homes.

Given such harsh and stressful conditions it was all the more impressive that grandad Maudesley's humour was always sharp, honed over many years of his own hardships and travel. He was especially cutting about those in closest proximity to him, like our neighbours. Life had always been tough in the East End but in the period between the wars, life was riven with misery. It was commonplace for distress and moaning to be accompanied openly by loud outbursts of tears from the ladies. Now grandad Maudesley was not a particularly uncaring person, but all the people faced tremendous hardships, and a liberal application of 'black humour' often enabled others only marginally more fortunate to get through the numerous crises of daily life. One of grandad's favourite exclamations to my grannie was, 'Jesus Christ Kate, that woman's got her bloody eyeballs connected to her bladder!' Other occasions he would be heard to mock 'You could boil bloody spuds in that woman's tears!'

In between the wars, East End family sizes gradually decreased but even in the 1930s it seemed that many of the children I mixed with, both at school and at home, were from families of at least six to eight people. Often boys and girls would arrive at school looking tired, unwashed and dishevelled. Their appearance was usually a sign of an overcrowded house and the almost certain fact that they had been bed sharing.

One of my best schoolboy pals was from a large family and he had to share a 3-foot bed with three of his brothers and sisters, sleeping head-to-toe. Two children would sleep at the head of the bed and the other two at the foot. Such a common arrangement was not conducive to sleep, as a battle would develop through the night over the share of the blanket. Cheesy feet and bed-wetting were also reasons for a bad nights sleep. With their outside WCs, the children were reluctant to get out of bed and go downstairs into the cold, being afraid of the dark. Even the chamber pot under the bed carried the risk of being stepped in during the night, and so many bed wettings occured.

Even with such chronic overcrowding I spent much of my boyhood in my grandparents' home while my mother strove to augment my father's lowly sea-going wages. The freedom that came with this child-minding arrangement meant I could spend more hours playing than I could have reasonably expected at my age and it gave me admission to the houses and flats of many of my street playmates. Some of these homes were poor in the extreme and cleanliness was obviously not a priority with most of them, having their own distinctive smell ranging from winter-green ointment to boiled cabbage or dried pee. With such a fussily clean grandmother and mother, the dirt, poverty and smells of some of those Canning Town homes were a shock to me and will be forever etched on my memory.

Due to the sheer scale of the dust and dirt, a market opened for the wildly fantastic invention, to us at least, of the vacuum cleaner. The first I saw were mostly cylindrical with a single brush attachment, called 'Goblins' and they retailed at 7s 6d. However, this fantastic invention had the effect of plunging even more people into the mire of debt. One ploy used by unscrupulous salesmen was to unpack a new cleaner and, after vacuuming the rug or settee, emptying its contents onto a sheet of newspaper to demonstrate its efficiency. However, if the householder wasn't impressed or simply couldn't afford it, the salesman would threaten to take the unhygienic evidence and show it to the neighbours, playing on 'pride over poverty'.

Whilst my grandmother's house was a restricted area as far as visitors were concerned, just a few doors away my aunt Flossie's place was a free house, where anyone was welcome – including the pushy vacuum-cleaning sales-men, and so she became one of the first owners of a 'Goblin'! I can recall being there with my cousin Joyce, plus various neighbours, watching with wide-eyed amazement as the chrome and black machine sucked up dirt and dust before our very eyes, but its roaring noise prevented anyone from hearing my uncle Jack arrive a bit worse for wear after a session at the 'Gog' public house. He was known to be prone to violent behaviour towards aunt Floss when drunk, and this knowledge caused everybody to make a hasty retreat before Jack kicked the cleaner and set about poor Floss (all eighteen-odd stone of her), ranting and raving for his dinner. She might not have shared the Maudesley trait of a spick and span home, but she was an easy-going soul and forgiving of husband Jack's occasional temper – the cause of a rift between her and the Maudesleys.

To relieve the humdrum life of the locals, and to give herself some hope, aunt Floss would invite a fortune teller round to her house to lighten, or often depress, the local women who assembled in the back kitchen. As they went individually into her front room for a reading, Joyce and I would sit on the stairs trying to hear the teller's predictions. Sometimes the group would sit holding half empty teacups for the fortune teller to read the tea leaves. I wonder what magic that fortune teller might dabble in now ... since the invention of the tea bag!

My dad's aunt Maud Bridges, lived in nearby Poplar in a dingy road of old terraced houses which I used to visit from time to time. It was close to the equally drab Queens Theatre – the East End's variety home renowned for its bawdy humour and nude tableaux plus third-rate supporting acts. To help supplement uncle Bob's meagre wages aunt Maud took in lodgers from the theatre. These were usually double acts and they were accommodated in the small second bedroom, her kids having to share the third bedroom. On one, never to be forgotten occasion, aunt Maud had a request to board five midgets from the theatre. Seeing a golden chance to make a bit of extra cash she per-suaded uncle Bob to give up their double bed for the week to accommodate the five dwarfs. I imagined the dwarfs slept 'two up and three down' in the big soft bed, just like in the fairytale book. On the second night aunt Maud decided to make a fine 'Cockney' stew for supper for the whole family, dwarfs included. The returning midgets ate the stew with relish but unfortunately with serious consequences. Their dwarfism required a strict diet and some of the rich stew's ingredients weren't on it! In the middle of the night all five of them had terrible attacks of the aptly named 'runs'. Aunt Maud's house was an old house with an outside 'carsey'. To make matters worse than they already were, the scullery door leading to the back yard was locked. The dwarfs could not control themselves resulting in an almighty and foul smelling mess to be made in the bed, all over the floor, trailing down the stairs and ending in a mass at the scullery door! I recall aunt Maud telling mum that it was the smell that had woken her rather than the screams of the desperate dwarfs! This particular 'golden opportunity' for making money resulted in her having to get rid of all the bedding at considerable cost. I understand that she told the Queens Theatre subsequently, 'Only couples' and 'No more bloody dwarfs!'

Me in November 1931, aged 27 months.

CHAPTER SIX

Between the Wars – Out in the Street

Pedal bikes were a frequent sight on our streets. The local midwife always used one and for much of my childhood I believed that babies came from her little 'black bag' mounted thereon. To a lesser extent, motorbikes were used and even lesser, cars. In fact the only motorised activity that seemed to interfere with our street games was the council dustcart. As the street was mostly always clear it became an undisputed playground for all the kids who lived there. The street was our second home.

Regular boyish pastimes included 'hoops and skimmers' which consisted of an old bike wheel rim which was rotated forward by a skimmer, fashioned from a piece of bent wire. The main aim of the game, besides wearing out boot leather, was to keep the hoop going straight ahead and on the move. Some children wouldn't go for errands for their parents without taking one along and the unmistakable tinny noise was heard down every street in my childhood.

Another fad was walking around on crude, homemade stilts. The possession of such stilts depended on the, legally or otherwise obtained, 2-by-2 inch wood quartering, with two blocks nailed halfway up their length on which to place one's feet. The spiked iron railings around some houses proved to be ideal support for mounting the stilts and to stop overbalancing.

In retrospect, it seems as if I spent the whole of my childhood playing in the street and warranting my mother's description of my being a 'street urchin'. But the streets were a fun place to be as well as safe from being run over and we felt little or no fear of being criminally assaulted or abducted in those long gone days.

In pre-war streets, one could mix freely and join in the many games that cost nothing. We all loved community skipping with a long piece of thick dockside rope stretched across the road from kerb to kerb and rotated by the other kids. We'd skip in and out, making sure not to get the rope caught up under our chins, causing a nasty graze or burn. Then there was Tin Can Tommy – a form of hide-and-seek in which a tin can would be banged on the ground when the one who was 'it' found their friend's hiding place.

We only needed some chalk and a stick of firewood or a pebble to play hopscotch. There were five stones (or Gobs) played, sitting in a group on the ground. The stones, that had to be small and differently coloured, would be in the palm of one hand and, in a pre-determined sequence, would be tossed a

'Stick 'em up Joyce!' – my cousin and I in the streets of the East End, 1935.

little way into the air and then caught on the back of that hand. This wasn't as easy as it sounds, especially as grabbing and catching was allowed.

The girls would do handstands against a wall, after tucking their frocks into their dark blue bloomers and vying for the chance to show who could remain with their legs in the air and feet against the wall the longest. Washing lines from the back garden would be used to show off our individual skipping skills before tying it to the top of a street corner lamppost and turning it into a dangerous swing as it would coil tightly around the post and, if we weren't careful, someone's neck! If we felt like a change, we would play in the local park on the swings and seesaws. We formed non-hostile street gangs and we would sit on opposite sides of our street territory in an attempt to stare out the opposition or exchange childish insults to see who could keep it up the longest. We also made dens out of old boxes, or tents from a piece of bed sheet fixed over the small gap between the house and its front railings.

In exchange for a 2 lb empty jam or pickle jar, one could get a ride on a roundabout which toured the streets, mounted on the back of a flat cart, pulled by an old horse. It seated about six children at a time and was mounted on old roller skates. The owner would propel it round with much shoving and grunting. Any kid caught nicking a jar from his collection, in order to gain a free ride, was given a swift back-hander.

Some of the older girls liked to organise a mock 'May Queen' procession. They dressed the unfortunate young 'Queen' in a variety of old lace curtains and chenille tablecloths filched from the ragbag or borrowed when Mum wasn't looking. The Queen's crown was fashioned out of a battered old enamel colander with weeds like dandelions, daisies or buttercups poked into its many holes. The majestic wand was a stick covered with discarded silver paper whilst the Royal Coach was the boy's barrow, made from a wooden box from the grocers. It was either mounted on two old pram wheels with wooden shafts, or on to the back of a piece of wide board. It used four wheels; one pair at the front that were able to swivel and the other pair fixed under the box, where the barrow's owner, or the May Queen, would sit. The entire contraption had to be propelled by another boy pushing and running, whilst the driver controlled its direction with his feet on either side of the swivelling front axle.

I reckon I must have been about eight years old when I first dreamt of playing cricket for England against Don Bradman and his Australian Test Team. Then I imagined myself playing international football for England and my local club – West Ham.

The back streets became our Lords for cricket, or our Wembley or Upton Park for football. Two unevenly matched ragamuffin teams differing greatly in age, size and skill, kicked balls of any shape or size towards the respective goals marked out by a pile of coats or jerseys, with the kerbstones on each side of the road delineating the touchlines.

I played many positions, from goalkeeper to centre forward, assuming the role of whoever was the star player of the day. Scores were astronomical and more like a rugby result; 36–28 was a regular score. It was common for 'Dixie Dean' or 'Stanley Matthews' (the football stars of their day) to score 6, 10 or even 15 goals before a game would end abruptly when the owner of the ball was called indoors by his mother or he had been upset and taken his ball home.

Street cricket was less popular, mainly because of broken windows by the sloggers. They would smash the threadbare old tennis ball with a bat fashioned out of an old piece of floorboard which had a piece of cycle wheel innertube pulled over the rough, carved handle. The wicket would sometimes be chalked onto a house wall. We developed an ingenious high-tech umpire – the ball would be soaked in a puddle so if the batsman missed and the ball hit the wicket, the wet splodge from the ball showed if he was in or out.

If cricket was played in the middle of the road then the wicket would be the nearest dustbin or a propped-up piece of board. Boundaries were considered to be about twenty houses in each direction from the wicket and if one had to run a mile to retrieve a long driven ball, then it was '6 and out'. I played for England in the single wicket 'Test Matches', batting as 'Len Hutton' or

'Dennis Compton'. Sometimes I would bowl as 'Larwood' or 'Bill Voce'. Whichever way around we played we always made sure we beat the Aussies.

The street ball games were fun times but often painful as my mother would scrub my tired skin and dirt encrusted knees with Vim – a household scouring powder. For the statistically minded, my highest goal-scoring feat in any one street football match was about ten, whilst at cricket I scored hundreds of runs and only broke one window, causing me to run like hell to avoid being caught.

On our street it was a regular sight to see rent and debt collectors, insurance men, street photographers taking pictures for a penny and Indian men selling Indian toffee or silks and linens from large, old, battered suitcases. There were tinkers pushing handcarts loaded with tin cooking utensils and other house-hold requirements, all of the cheap and nasty variety, the winkle man with his tin bathtubs and enamel bowls full of sea food, barrel organists, often with a bad tempered rhesus monkey, collecting money and, on my street, an old lady named Aunt Etty who sold chocolates from a perambulator that was even older than her. Then, at that magical time that came only once a day during the summer, the ice-cream trike with its dark blue box carrying the slogan 'Stop me and buy one!' The seller would announce his arrival with a constant ringing of his tinny bell and I, like all the other kids on the street, dreamt of that moment every single night.

Usually on a Friday night and Saturday lunchtime, the Pie and Crumpet man would appear, balancing a large baker's tray on his head and ringing a school-type assembly bell. My grandfather said it was because he was a head-master, not because he was associated with the school, but because of his skill in swivelling his head without the tray changing direction if someone called him from behind. As his visits coincided with payday for the local labour force, he did a roaring trade outside the nearby public houses *The Peacock* and *The Gog*. The majority of dockworkers believed that a seven-course meal was a meat pie and six pints of ale!

Except for celebrating Royal occasions, the most eagerly awaited annual event was always Guy Fawkes Night. This was a chance for my friends and me to make a little bit of money, just as we had seen the street traders do. For weeks previously, wood was scrounged and stored in backyards and 'Guys' were made from any clothing that was far beyond further use. They would then be paraded on an old pram or kid's barrow with each group begging, 'Penny for the Guy'. They waited expectantly outside the dock gates, pubs or tram stops where drunks were so far gone they showered the beggars with what little was left of their ale money. Large bonfires would be built in the middle of the road in complete disregard for the damage they would cause to the closely-packed houses and the gas and water services running below. Because of the shortage of money and the fear of them going up in smoke, there was a limited selection of fireworks, but those available were joyously ignited simultaneously with the ritual burning of the 'Guy'.

I came home early from school one 5th November to find the most magnificent 'Guy' I had ever seen. It had bangers in its mouth, rockets in its hat and held a large cascade of fireworks in its hands. At first I was overwhelmed and then terrified as it started to move. It edged towards me, slowly, waving its newspaper-stuffed arms. I was beginning to wonder if I would live to score another goal on our paved pitch when my uncle Alf, unable to contain his laughter, stepped out of the 'Guy' suit with an enormous grin. Though relieved to still be alive, I was slightly disappointed.

Some children used this ruse whilst collecting on bonfire night until, in the thirties, a man, probably drunk, stabbed a young boy dressed as a 'Guy' as he tried to see if he was real or stuffed. Stern warnings were given out at School Assembly not to dress up as 'Guys' in future.

Winter in the streets

I believe the only time I saw our street really clean was early one winter morning. An overnight blanket of snow had fallen and I saw it before it turned into brown and black slush by the thaw, the pedestrians, the horse and carts or the odd motor vehicle. But even without the people and machines the snow would have rapidly taken on a top dressing of black soot from the many factories around. In those days cinder-ash was cheaper than salt so housewives would liberally apply it over the pavement in front of their houses, so adding to the filth that the snow had temporarily camouflaged. We kids enjoyed, in traditional fashion, our own winter sports. We made dangerous slides along the pavements or school playground and giant snowballs of more than a yard diameter, made by rolling them around in the unspoiled patches of snow. Snowball fights were 'Battles Royal' against the next street. The aim was to protect oneself by nicking the first dustbin lid one could find (they were nearly always left outside the front doors) to use as a shield. In Saturday cinema newsreels we saw the rich out in Switzerland, skiing and curling, and being hauled around in great sleighs; but we weren't envious. Holidays abroad, winter or summer, were for the well-off and to be tanned brown was considered by Eastenders the mark of an outdoor labourer!

Shopping

Shopping in my childhood days was not as expansive, or expensive, as it is now. This was partly due to lack of shops and limited variety of goods but lack of money was also a major factor. There were the small corner shops in the back streets, or the slightly larger shops in the High Street and these were mainly for food and drink. Pawnshops were popular with their 'three brass balls' trade sign, as well as shops for cat's meat, paraffin oil, hardware, corn chandlers, second-hand clothes, furniture, newspapers, tobacco, and sweets.

The 'fast food' shops of the day were Manzes pie and mash shops, where savoury meat pies were served with mashed potatoes swimming in liquor; a thick, lumpy gravy which was either bright-green (parsley based) or dark-brown (base questionable!).

Butchers opened all hours, selling pease pudding, faggots, and saveloys before ending the week on a Saturday night with an auction of meat. General grocers were considered little goldmines as they traded in a wide variety of foodstuffs and other day-to-day household necessities. Usually along the counter front would be a row of square, open-topped tins holding an assortment of biscuits into which you could rummage with your grimy fingers. Colourful packaging, or indeed hygiene were not obligatory at that time!

There were a few local 'sell everything' department stores, which no longer exist, having risen and fallen in the boom and bust history of the area. They were known for their overhead-wire system along which, small, cylindrical containers holding the customer's money would be propelled by an unseen force. They would race at high speed from the counter to a centrally located cashier who would return the cylinder with receipt and change.

Eagerly awaited annual treats, if you were really lucky, were to the big stores in Oxford Street and Holborn – Selfridges and Gamages. The latter's toy department was like an Aladdin's cave for children. Sainsbury's in those days had a few small shops which sold groceries on a small-scale and boasted a good selection of cooked meats. Marks and Spencer arrived in nearby East Ham High Street North, selling only clothes. The popular shops preceding the Sainsbury's chain was the Home and Colonial, where I would watch in wide-eyed amazement at straw-hatted, striped-aproned shop assistants taking butter from a large box and expertly patting it with two wooden spatulas into half-pound blocks. Street markets on Rathbone Street (E16) and Queens Road (E13), sold groceries, meat, livestock, clothes and fascinating live eels, which slithered around in tanks, doomed to their fate, waiting to be selected by hungry customers.

To supplement the shops and the street markets, there were many traders who trudged the streets with their wares, exchanging old clothes or bric-a-brac for a piece of china. The 'any old iron or lumber' dealer, the horsemeat man and the rag and bone man were all regular sights. There was the Sunday morning winkle man's cart and 'Grooms' baker's cart, both of which were very welcome by those who grew rhubarb – man, woman and child eagerly dashing out to scoop up the valuable manure the horses left behind, in whatever recepticle they could find, often still steaming hot!

In a back yard, which ran alongside the pavement of a road adjoining ours, a woman known as 'Gypsy Nell' had dozens of wild rabbits hanging from a rope line, ready for the pot. The flies and the smell would today have caused it to be closed by the Health Authorities, but at a 'tanner' a time it was a cheap meal. I don't remember any cases of salmonella or bacterial poisoning being heard of; perhaps germs really were scared off by carbolic soap smells?

There were no betting shops, since off-course betting of any sort was illegal but that didn't stop the unofficial bookmakers making 'a bob or two' anyway. They would employ a runner to collect bets on street corners, or outside certain shops, at a time unknown to the police. There was often great excitement if the police carried out a raid aimed at catching a runner, but they were a protected species and would disappear through the door of the nearest house without any fear of being caught. Gambling, like smoking and drinking, was a way of life. I was always amazed at how mostly uneducated men could not only write out a bet, but as they scanned the racing results in the Stop Press of the '*Star*', could work out to the nearest ha'penny what a bet would bring them. Natural 3R's education at work!

Pubs, more commonly known as beer shops, were strategically placed on street corners or on the routes home from the docks or Fords Dagenham car works. Old ladies would often be seen in *The Peacock*, wearing flat caps and crocheted shawls, peeling vegetables or shelling peas for supper whilst supping a pint of Stout or Porter.

One night as I waited for my grandfather and my dad to come out of 'The Peacock', there was pandemonium when a beggar with a pet rhesus monkey went around the tables collecting money. Unfortunately for the monkey, it knocked a docker's beer over (an unforgiveable crime), and in revenge the docker put his lighted cigarette up the monkey's rear end, causing it to take off across the bar and knocking down all the bottles of spirits, whilst simultaneously scaring the hell out of the barmaid, who ran screaming from the pub, followed by the monkey and its owner.

As a young boy, one of my regular weekend errands was going to the 'Cherry Tree', a local public house to fetch grandad's weekend treats; 3 pints of beer. Grandad always demanded this be brought in his own bottles. These were the trademark square 'Johnnie Walker' whisky bottles. He found these easier to hold, bragging to people that 'as old as I am I don't need glasses!' then with his customary short pause adding wittingly, 'I always drink out of the bottle!'

It was on one hot Sunday dinner time – we never called it 'lunch' in those days – I was on my way back when I felt the overwhelming urge for a cold drink. I swigged at one of the bottles to slake my thirst. It was great. But as in a flash my thirst quenched, I realised grandad would see the missing beer. Afraid that I would get a good ticking off, I frantically searched for somewhere to refill the bottle. Horses were still standard transport in those days and the streets were dotted with large granite horse troughs. I was saved! I dipped the short ration beer bottle into the local horse trough covering my crime. Having watched grandad consume his weekly beer 'ration' many times, I knew he always drank the first and sometimes the second in a non-stop guzzling motion. I made sure that the diluted bottle was given to him first. Sure enough he guzzled at such speed that he never noticed the difference, which says a lot for the beer of the day or the quality of the horse trough waters!

Holidays in the 1930s – hop picking!

In the pre-war days of my childhood it was only the well-off that could afford holidays. The remainder of the population laboured hard in return for such poor reward that made the taking of holidays impossible, thereby dictating that cheaper, or preferably free, alternatives be sought. But hope for us holiday-deprived East Enders came via Kent's hop famers who were striving to satisfy the burgeoning demands of the Home Counties brewers to supply quality ale at an affordable price to the working classes, in lieu of the more expensive wines and spirits that were the preferred 'tipple' of the rich.

In the 30s, the agricultural excellence of the Kent soil was found to be particularly suited to the growing of hops so that vast areas of the Kent countryside were given over to their planting as the demand for beer grew. However, whilst the hop vines were comparatively easy to grow, they were labour intensive to harvest, so causing the hop farmers to go for cheap, short-term labour. And where better to look for such readily available labour than in the poor and high unemployment market of nearby London's East End. The particular area of this labour search was not, however, concentrated on hiring men for the job, but women, especially the working class mums. These oft downtrodden women were offered, and gratefully accepted, a break from their daily docklands and industrial environment away from 'the old man' (well, during the week, that was!) and the chance to earn some much needed money.

The annual migration of mums and their kids from London to the hopfields around Biddenden, Paddock Wood, Goudhurst and Headcorn areas of Kent, became part of East End folklore. Commonly known as 'going hopping', it became the only holiday that most of us East Enders could, or would ever likely go on, throughout our humdrum lives. But it too was hard work and in living conditions which nowadays equate to those standards found in Far Eastern third world countries. The accommodation, which was sited adjacent to the hopfields, was very basic, consisting of a hut about the size of a seaside beach hut made from corrugated iron which, when it rained and picking of hops stopped, became a noisy, boring 'prison cell'. The farmer supplied each family with a load of straw to stuff a linen mattress cover which was placed on a wooden platform to become an uncomfortable bed. Some of the regular pickers took their own feather filled eiderdown or flock filled mattress to sleep more peacefully on. Tea chests and baskets that had been packed with all our clothing and utensil needs for the whole stay, were placed underneath the primitive beds that were made up each day top-to-tail with the mum and small child at the head and older kids at the foot. At weekends the 'the old man' would often arrive, and the sleeping arrangements would be rearranged to suit.

Lighting and cooking was by paraffin lamps and Primus stoves and although there was a communal cold water tap there were no WCs. There was only a small single-seater loo with a plank seat placed over a large, smelly bucket that was often too heavy for mum to lift and had to be left for the farmer or a weekend dad to empty. The farm would often stock essentials like bread, milk, margarine and some vegetables, but other groceries had to be bought from the village shop whose owner would be so pleased to see and serve us pickers because in this once-a-year period we spent more than his regular local customers. The big appetites caused by working in the fresh air had to be satisfied by anything which we could boil or fry on the Primus stove, or on the bonfire made outside the hut: stews, boiled suet pudding, hock of bacon, sausages and mash, and eggs and bacon were the dishes of my hop picking 'holidays'.

Our hop pickers' day started early, being up at 6am with a 'cat's lick and promise' (in lieu of a proper wash with soap and hot water), then breakfast and be ready to pick at about 7.00am. Each group was allocated a picking area and a hop bin, which was formed by sacking nailed to two 6-feet long poles, like a deep baggy stretcher, supported at each end by 'X' frames. When the bin was full, a couple of farm labourers carried away the 'stretcher' for its contents to be measured into bushels, for which we were paid at a rate of five bushels for a shilling (five pence today).

Before picking began, the 'binds' (as the strung up vines were known) had to be pulled down from the network of strings through which the vines had weaved their way to reach the top of the forest of stout poles some twelve to fifteen feet high. If it had been raining, or there had been a heavy early morning dew, the pulling of the binds usually resulted in a soaking for us. The women would sit at the side of the hop bin for up to four hours at a time, mostly without a break, laying the binds along the bin's length to make the picking of the hops easier and letting them drop directly into the bin. If the mum's daily labour was to be rewarded in full, then it had to be for 'clean' bushels which meant not letting too many leaves fall in. Because we children had smaller and more flexible fingers, we were able to pick the binds more cleanly without getting any leaves in the bin and sometimes the farmer's men would encourage us by treating us to a few sweets.

In our 'off' time we used to play around the fields in complete safety, except when we were chased off by an irate farmer's wife, or dogs, for scrumping the abundance of fruit from the many orchards which surrounded the hop-fields. Those carefree happy days, soon to be disrupted by the onset of war, were remembered long after our sun-tanned cockney skins had returned to white and our black stained fingers from picking the hops had faded away.

Credit and Pawn

Credit or 'tick' was often a way of life in the docklands area. 'Tick' became the poor shopper's byword that enabled them to get by on a week-to-week basis. It was common to ask the grocer to put it on the 'slate' until the family bread-winner could hand over at least part of his wages before he boozed or bet it away. Most grocery shops had a large notice over the counter which pro-claimed, 'Please do not ask for credit as refusal often offends!' These warnings became necessary for shopkeepers who did not want to end up in the poor and sorry state of their customers.

For those who couldn't afford to pay cash at a shop, there were always 'Tally Men', who operated a credit system allowing the poor to live as they would have liked if only they had the money. They acted as agents for the large stores, selling goods with a small down-payment but high weekly repayments, until the debt was cleared. Tally Men certainly had their work cut out trying to collect their weekly dues and many of them were reputed to have prematurely aged and died of worry.

There was also the Provident Cheque lady who ran a weekly club-card scheme. The amount granted on a store cheque depended on the customer's reliability but averaged at about 50s ($£2.50$). 'Tick', later known as Hire Purchase (HP), was more humorously known as buying goods on the 'glad and sorry' – glad you've got it but sorry you've got to pay for it.

The Pawnshop was an institution spoken of only in whispers. These premises were among the few financial pools in which the poor could dive in head first; ironically drowning themselves in debt. It seems incredible now that whole areas of people could exist by pawning something on a Monday and redeeming it at a little extra cost the following Friday. They would repeat the process each week, so keeping themselves afloat.

The poor had to keep diving into that whirlpool, not because they wanted to, but because they were forced to. Those unfortunate enough not to be able to redeem their goods would stare disbelievingly through the Pawnbrokers window under the sign 'Unredeemed Pledge'. The Pawnbroker would make a handsome profit, especially with jewellery, whilst the hard-working man could do nothing but glare at the objects he once held in his own hands. In the window of Gregory's Pawn Shop, just outside the Victoria Dock Gates, the pawnbroker's sad collection was brightened by a bizarre array of pairs of false teeth and spectacles, as unredeemed pledges!

The pawnshop rules were strict. Whatever was pledged had to be clean and potentially re-saleable at a good profit. My mother once spoke about a neighbour calling after her husband on his way out on a Saturday night in his one and only suit, 'Watch those beer stains now and mind you don't lean against anything sticky or tear it!' That wife had good reason for her bellowed warning – the old man was going out on next week's housekeeping and his clean suit had to be pawned at 8.00 am sharp on Monday morning.

The financial balance in playing the 'Tally Man' and Pawnbroker against each other was delicate; rather like 'robbing Peter to pay Paul'. It required clever timing. With many people owning only the clothes they stood up in, it was an ever recurring problem to get something to pawn and to that end, this credit system used by big department stores came in useful. With store cheques the shops not only ensured that any available money was spent with them, but it gave people a chance to purchase something that would enable them to get on the 'rob Peter to pay Paul money-go-round'.

The downward financial spiral into debt was, thankfully for some, halted by the declaration of war, the ensuing German Blitz and resultant evacuation. This gave many debtors the chance to flee without leaving a forwarding address, so abdicating their responsibility to pay outstanding personal debts.

Births, Marriages, Deaths

In my boyhood, the locals loved occasions, any occasions which broke the monotony, particularly Royal Anniversaries but anyone's wedding, an ambulance call or even death were all rather public affairs. Neighbours would congregate outside whichever house was hosting the event. Post wedding and funeral parties were always held in the house rather than in a hall and the confines of these small houses dictated that the number of guests invited were kept to a minimum. I don't remember any couple going away on honeymoon; most, due to their financial circumstances, were back to work on the following Monday.

On Royal occasions, through school, we would be given a commemorative 3d or 6d piece and street parties would be organised for the day. Two occasions I remember were King George V's Silver Jubilee in 1935 and the aborted coronation of King Edward VIII in 1937. However, due to the latter's abdication, the programmed school and street celebrations were postponed until the coronation of King George VI. Red, white and blue were very evident in the bunting-bedecked classroom and streets and a carnival atmosphere prevailed. Roads were closed to allow the schoolchildren to enjoy a terrific bun fight, races were run and impromptu junior talent shows were set up. Dining tables formed a stage and someone's old piano was dragged on as an all-night party ensued. Celebrations were simple and community-driven affairs.

There was a great stigma attached to out-of-wedlock pregnancies in the pre-war years. I remember poor Lilly Nichols who used to walk me to school up to her leaving at 14. A couple of years later an ambulance drew up to her house. A body was brought out through a throng of nosey neighbours who would always gather for funerals, weddings or an ambulance! The body was that of poor desperate Lilly. Unbeknown to me Lilly had become pregnant at just 16 and was of course unmarried. This was a serious issue and the source of much disgrace which could force a family out and into ruination in those still strongly 'Victorian' times. Lilly unfortunately had an 'old goat' of a father and could not face the shame she would bring upon the family. Rather than tell anyone and in absolute fear of her father, Lilly drank a bottle of 'Lysol', a well known brand of strong carbolic disinfectant. Lilly suffered an agonizing, but relatively quick solution to her disgrace – death. Some other teenage girls who became pregnant were sent to Goodmayes, a local asylum for the mentally disturbed where they were incarcerated for many years. Many suffered horrendously, becoming mentally disturbed in the process, but the guilty men got away with it. In those male dominated times, 'it takes two' was conveniently forgotten.

Putting pride before poverty each week families would make payments of a penny or ha'penny to insurance agents or 'Clubs', to preclude the indignity of a pauper's funeral. Contributors wanted desperately to show family pride with an elegant funeral carriage drawn by sleek, black horses, crowned with black feather plumes on their tossing heads. These magnificent beasts would impatiently paw the road with their polished hooves whilst snorting and dribbling white froth from their mouths. They would wait for the coffin to be slid into the hearse and for mourners to take their place in the accompanying carriages, before moving off slowly and majestically to the East London Cemetery for burial. Cremation was almost unheard of in those days and was frowned upon as an alien custom.

As horse-drawn carriages became more expensive and the motor car started to find its way into public acceptance, the horses were replaced by Daimler cars. They lacked the same appeal as the elegant carriages and would merit only a passing glance from the locals. The pomp and ceremony of plumed black horses, with their royal purple saddlecloths, would cause people to come out and watch the passing procession.

Out of respect, the neighbours of the deceased would lower their wooden-slat Venetian blinds for a week whilst, in the bereaved home, the wireless and the gramophone would stay silent until after the burial. Almost without exception the body of the deceased would be returned to the house within a couple of days to 'lie in state' in the parlour that was darkened by the closed blinds and made sombre by the burning of a candle, the draping of black cloth over the front room mirror and the smell of eau-de-cologne. The coffin would be completely, or at least half, open and the face of the deceased covered with a lace square. Neighbours gathered outside and the family sat in silence until the undertaker arrived.

Whatever the local's plight, they would ensure that no matter what, the event would the best they could afford. I was always amazed at the large and lavish graves, tombs or vaults scattered around the East London cemetery. A regular Sunday afternoon out, before coming home to bread and butter, winkles and watercress, was a trip to the cemetery to change the flowers and show respect at the place where many of my forebears had been interred. I would stand and gaze in sadness at the befitting monument to the thirty-eight people who had been drowned at the launch of HMS *Albion* from the Thames Ironworks in 1898. The tragedy occurred when the precarious public platform on which onlookers were standing to watch the launch crumbled. The victims were swept into the water by the wash from the ship as it left the slipway. The road leading to the East London Cemetery was Hermit Road and, at its junction with Barking Road, stood Trinity Church, circa 1867. The church became famous in Victorian times for inspiring the popular music hall song of the day, 'At Trinity Church I met my doom!' Bus and tram conductors would often sing the first few bars of the song instead of calling out the stop outside the church. It survived the Blitz but unfortunately not the post-war planners.

One of the most feared men to visit the streets during the pre-war years was the School Board Man. If a child had been absent from school for more than three days without proof of sickness or accident, then the home of that child would be visited and explanations sought.

Truancy, or 'bunking off' as we called it, was very rare and would result in the culprit being caned across the palm of the hand. In addition to this physical punishment and for any other punishment, no matter how trivial, the incident would be recorded in the school's Punishment Book and reputedly reappeared on one's Character Reference when leaving school. A serious issue in those days!

As we all have done at some point in our lives, we feigned sickness in its many forms, in order to get a day off. Then we would make a rapid and miraculous recovery the moment all our friends were safely behind their desks. I often tried using that ploy and my mother would send me off the next day excusing my absence with my having a 'bilious attack' – a quasi-medical term she had copied from our family Bible, but had no idea what it was; but neither did the teacher!

A more 'genuine' opportunity to bunk off school presented itself one day. Grandad always had a pipe on the go. Whether it was lit or not didn't seem to matter to him. He just sucked away at the stem probably as he had done most of his life. It was filled with acrid smelling twist tobacco – a very strong plug tobacco essentially for chewing and much favoured by seamen. It came in coils some two feet long, about ½″ thick by 1 ½″ wide and usually kept in the shop in an old round cake tin, being unwound from within like a black shiny snake and cut into half- or one-ounce pieces from which the smoker cut small chips to load the pipe bowl. When finally lit after umpteen matches had been sacrificed, the initial puffs would cause a great deal of coughing from the smoker and any passive smokers who were unlucky enough to be in range. I was about

8 or 9 when one day coming home at dinner time straight to his house I noticed his cap and pipe on the scullery table. Trying to impersonate him I donned the cap and stuck the pipe in my mouth and sucked; hard! I almost died on the spot as I choked, coughed, splattered and was violently sick. Grandad hearing the commotion, slapped me hard on the back encouraging me to 'Bring it up cock, it might be a gold watch!' I managed to escape school for the rest of the week so at least there was some benefit. But no; my teacher asked me to explain my mum's sick note covering my absence. Reluctantly I stood up and explained what I had done to my classmates. The teacher proudly held me up to the rest of the class as an example of what happens to under-age smokers. Needless to say, I never used that method again to bunk-off school, nor to impersonate grandad!

As a boy in elementary school, there was a rigidly imposed discipline, which more often than not included a physical punishment. 'Four-handers' were an occasional occurrence – two strokes of the cane on each hand. Such an incident notoriously sent me rushing to back to my seat, to grip the iron legs of my desk to cool down my burning palms. Teachers held absolute power and you answered back at your peril. We sat at neat rows of battered and scarred wooden desks, each with a flip top lid and an ink well in the corner. Inside we placed our books and sandwiches if we had any. A neat little hole was drilled into one corner to let out 'schoolboy detrius', though I recall my friend thinking it was obviously perfectly suited for exposing his penis to unsuspecting girls!

There were no school dinners, except for the poorest, who were humiliatingly handed their free dinner tickets on a daily basis. As this was done ritually in front of the whole class, it encouraged segregation of 'them' and 'us'. These children were also given a free pair of black lace-up boots every six months, each of which had a hole punched into the upper ankle part to prevent the boots being pawned. Another humiliation, inflicted only on the boys, was to have their hair close-cropped (also known as a 'Tuppenny all over'). However, a two-inch fringe was left over the forehead, as it was believed to be necessary to prevent the breeding of head lice. These poor boys were given the nickname of 'Chequer baldhead'.

School milk, a third-of-a-pint at a ha'penny, was served every morning but was not compulsory. If you were clever enough to save your money, you could convert it later in the local sweet shop, which was far more appealing.

Outside school, boys were encouraged to join the local Cub and Scouts Troops or the Boys Brigade. There weren't many alternatives. We had one Victorian public indoor swimming pool but later, in about 1936, an open-air lido was built and proved a great summer attraction. For those families who couldn't have a bath, for whatever reason, there was a local bath-house. It had well-worn grotty bath cubicles where an outside attendant controlled the water. On entry, a piece of un-perfumed soap and an inadequate linen towel was provided. In-bath discipline was strict, especially if the duty attendant was one who sadistically enjoyed turning the taps continuously from hot and cold. A father could take a couple of his children in at one time but you had to be over fourteen to be allowed in to bathe alone. They had great fun shouting requests from their own cubicle for 'more cold water' for a completely different cubicle number and then waiting for the yells from the unsuspecting bather. The only time I used the bath-house was on the way home from the local football pitch in a mud-splattered state. I jumped in the bath with all my football gear still on so my mum wouldn't nag me for getting dirty.

School sports, like football and cricket, were played with pride and passion against other local schools. If selected to play for any of the school teams it was considered a great honour and deserving of respect from all one's classmates. For football there were no goal nets; just posts, and the ball was a bladder-lined leather one which, when wet, was so heavy it would almost pile-drive a person into the ground if headed. Shin pads consisted of exercise books stuffed down our dad's old socks and boots were made of stiff leather that took about six matches and many blisters before they were 'broken-in'. A weekly application of 'Dubbin' to soften the leather was not much help.

The school's cricket bag contained just two pads, both for the wicketkeeper if we were fielding, or one each on the forward leg of the two boys at the crease when batting. Two antique bats bound with insulating tape to repair the splits in the bat's edges, six stumps, two bails and a 'conker' ball (a hard composition ball without an outer casing) completed the sorry set. On one of my few appearances in the First XI, versus the formidable St Lukes, I was top scorer with 3 out of a team total of 11. For the rest of that day, I was treated as if I was one of Britain's great sporting heroes.

I showed more promise academically than I did on the sports field, though I did come first in the egg and spoon race in the school's sports day in the Summer of 1939. I won a canvas and leather haversack. Life as a child was pretty idyllic even in the East End in that summer. But things were soon to change. My new, hard-won haversack, unexpectedly came in useful when I had to carry my personal belongings on evacuation from the London docks area on 1st September; just two days before the outbreak of the Second World War.

CHAPTER SEVEN

From Peace to War

Preparing for War

Almost a year before the commencement of hostilities between Britain and Germany, in late September 1938, the threat of war was seemingly all around us: the Phoney War had begun.

The year 1939 sticks out in my memory as a year of expectancy for war – a year of fear. The path from the ill-fated Anglo-German talks in Munich, 1938, through the 'phoney war' (1938–40) was bumpy and uncertain. Following Germany's incorporation of Austria into the Third Reich, demands were made for part of Czechoslovakia. This caused British Prime Minister, Neville Chamberlain, to meet German Chancellor, Adolf Hitler to discuss the war threat in Europe. He returned with what would prove to be a worthless document, the 'Munich Agreement'. Chamberlain used Disraeli's phrase to validate the success of his mission – 'Peace with Honour' and to declare 'I believe it is peace for our time'. How wrong he proved to be.

In the spring of 1939, Mussolini occupied Albania and Hitler seized Czechoslavakia. The world and the pubs and streets of the East End wondered if Poland would be next. This possibility prompted Chamberlain to make a stand by going against Hitler's quest for European domination, joining with France to protect Polish territory against aggression. A few months later Hitler demanded Danzig and the Polish Corridor, which since the First World War had separated East Prussia from the rest of Germany. In August 1939, Hitler made another non-aggression pact. This time it was with Josef Stalin.

Trenches were being dug in our public parks to serve as air-raid shelters and over 30 million gas masks were issued to men, women and children. Huge barrage balloons billowed in the skies above and around us and plans were being laid for the mass evacuation of civilians. The temporary reprieve gained by Neville Chamberlain from his meeting with Adolf Hitler in Munich was, however, soon to recede as Hitler proceeded regardless of any treaty with Britain. The spectre of war loomed large as gas masks, air-raid precautions (ARP), blackout preparations and the fear of attacks from the air by the Luftwaffe (who had honed their aerial combat and bombing skills by participating in the Spanish civil war a few years earlier) became increasingly familiar features of my everyday life as September 1939 approached. Re-armament became a priority, especially for the RAF to bring their fighter squadrons up to strength with new Hurricanes and Spitfires, to combat the Luftwaffe threat.

In the national press there was an alarmist trend as it was reported that the Luftwaffe might launch an overwhelming attack on London, frequently referred to as the 'knock out blow'. Air Staff calculated that the German planes could deliver some 700 tonnes of bombs a day and each ton could cause at least fifty casualties. With such doom laden statistics being fed to them, the Home Office estimated that in the first three months of such an air attack approximately 60,000,000 square feet of coffin timber would be needed just to bury the dead. Conscious of the high cost and the 'waste' of timber, tens of thousands of collapsible papier-mâché and cardboard coffins were stock-piled. It was then assumed within Government circles that in such a situation, civilian morale would crack under attack from the air and widespread panic would ensue, as hordes of Londoners would attempt to flee the shattered capital into the countryside. However, the government had not reckoned upon the spirit of the indefatigable Londoners and us East Enders in particular.

At the start of the war there were approximately 1½ million Civil Defence personnel, who were mostly voluntary and even at the height of the Blitz only 16,000 of London's 200,000 air-raid wardens were full time, paid at the lowly rate of £3 a week. To the general public the air-raid warden was unpopular and our attitude towards him ranged from mild amusement at his blue overalls and tin helmet, to open hostility. Before the Blitz started the warden was often regarded as a self-appointed 'Peeping Tom' who peered through people's blackout curtains for his own amusement.

Our local councils of East and West Ham, mindful of the Government's doomsday predictions, as well as to alleviate the burden being imposed on the rates, appealed to us all to help with civil defence by erecting our own air-raid shelters when they were delivered. These shelters, known as Anderson shelters after their designer Dr David A. Anderson, consisted of fourteen sheets of a heavy gauge corrugated steel forming a shell 6 feet high, 4½ feet wide and 6 feet long. We had to bury it a depth of 4 feet and then cover it with at least 15 inches of soil. It accommodated up to six people in conditions of cold, dank discomfort and was liable to regular flooding. The shelter was issued free to all those earning less than £5 a week and a charge of £7 for those with higher incomes. Unfortunately less than a third of the population had gardens big enough to benefit from their provision and the cramped back-yards of many an East End house were simply not big enough. Eventually about 2¼ million were erected and many of them survived the war to be sold as scrap or, more commonly, used as garden sheds.

Gas masks, which had been issued to us all by the time of the Munich crisis in September 1938, were distributed by thousands of voluntary workers whose communal effort was to characterise the Home Front during the war years. The fear of a gas attack was very real as there were thousands of ex-servicemen

The arrival in a London street of Anderson air-raid shelters in the immediate pre-war years. These 6 ft × 4 ft galvanised corrugated steel shelters had to be partly buried in the garden and covered with 15 inches of soil. Issued free to all those earning less than £250 per year, those on a higher income had to pay £7. They made cold, damp, and unhygienic bedrooms in the long cold nights of the blitz.

from the First World War; living reminders of the horrors of gas attacks on the Western Front in 1917–18. For me and many others the sensation of clammy breathlessness and smell of rubber and disinfectant was the first intimation of the approaching war. The gas masks, in original cardboard boxes or purpose-made cases, were a common sight everywhere and no one left home without one. Those under the age of five happily took to the special 'Mickey Mouse' gas masks designed to give this macabre precaution the appearance of a game whilst for babies, a small airtight chamber was provided through which filtered air was pumped, via bellows, by the mother.

The next stage of preparation for us was the blackout restrictions and the importance of this measure was widely displayed and the penalties for disobeying them listed. After gas mask rehearsals came the practice blackout, which was all very amusing to a young lad like me, and I couldn't wait for the war to start to wear my gas mask all day and walk around in the dark at night. I was soon to learn otherwise. Following the mock blackout, its procedure was modified and we then saw the Council workmen out in force, painting white bands round all posts, boxes and other obstacles along important streets and picking out kerbs and crossroads with white markings. All traffic lights and street lamps were fitted with blackout shields, allowing only a small cross of light to be seen instead of the usual full circle. All vehicles, including the popular bike, had to have shielded front and rear lamps and torches had to be masked. Everyone, except the blind, cursed the blackout.

Evacuation

The two abiding memories of the war remain, for me, my evacuation from London, along with thousands of others considered at risk and the German 'Blitzkrieg' which followed aimed at wiping me, my family, friends and the entire East End off the map. Both, in different ways, were traumatic not only for me but for so many others similarly caught up in the upheaval.

Just two days before the declaration of war the Government set in motion mass evacuation of mothers and children from 'at risk' areas. It wasn't a uniform operation across the country and places like Plymouth, Bristol and Swansea were not designated as high risk evacuation areas. Most of these supposedly safe cities were important ports so naturally they were heavily bombed during the first few weeks of the war, sending many evacuees scurrying back to the 'safety' of home in the East End. Nor did all the 'priority cases' choose to be evacuated, as evidenced in London where less than half the capital's schoolchildren were evacuated, a proportion reflected across the nation. Even so, the Minister of Health at this time likened the evacuation to 'an exodus bigger than that of Moses!' Evacuation provided photographers with some of the most evocative images of the early war years: heart rending pictures of tearful little children, labels hanging around their necks, gas mask holders strung from their scrawny shoulders, teddy-bears and dolls of all shapes and sizes clutched in their grubby little hands, their lips quivering with a mixture of excitement and apprehension. For almost all of them it was a bewildering experience, alone perhaps for the first time. I should know because I was one of them.

The reason for my particular evacuation was that the 'Royal' group of docks in east London, where I lived, would be highly likely to become strategic targets for the German Luftwaffe, therefore placing the local inhabitants at high risk. When the time eventually came for the evacuation, it was for so many of us the very first time that we had been away without at least one parent. I spent my tenth birthday in Russell Road School Evacuation Centre being prepared for what I thought was to be a holiday, gathered in classrooms and grouped only by age; each of us wearing around our necks the obligatory gas mask and a tie-on label showing our full names, date of births and home addresses, together with our ration books and Identity Cards. For two weeks we waited day after day for the order to move, not knowing where we were going or if we were ever again to see our mothers, who hovered daily at the school gates to say their last goodbyes. Whole schools were evacuated together to a 'secret' destination that even had we known its name we would be ignorant of wherever it was, since to most of us the known world only went as far as Southend, Margate or the hop-fields of Kent. Travelling in a fleet of red buses away from Custom House, my feelings were a mixture of fear and excitement as we reached one of the London rail terminals.

All the older boys and girls were enlisted to look after small groups of us younger children during the journey from the school gates to our final destination and were very bossy as they assumed the role of teachers, ordering us on and off the buses, onto the rail platform and into the waiting steam train. Unlike single-compartment trains, which I had only ever been on, this was a corridor train with a lavatory at the end. Most of the seating had been removed, forcing us to sit either on the floor or on our cases or bags, whilst the few seats remaining were grabbed by our 'carers'. When we moved off there was an excited rush for the windows to see where we were going and, for the whole length of the train, small heads were crammed together poking out of every window. Many of those children, with eyes tightly closed, wanting to feel the rush of 'fresh air' upon their faces, soon retreated to the safety of their compartment for a 'spit wash' after they were taunted about their blackened faces, caused by the foul smelling and sooty smoke from the steam engine's chimney. To keep out the belching fumes, a teacher ordered the windows to be kept shut and for us to 'settle down'. By then the excitement of adventure had started to wane and laughter was replaced by tears as we realised that not only had our travelling rations gone, but we wouldn't be going home for tea that day or perhaps any other day. There was an awful feeling of loneliness and fear of the unknown.

In most cases we kids arrived dirty, dishevelled, tired and obviously distressed, to find that wartime foster parents were only prepared to accept the most clean looking and tidily turned out of us. I am sure that many of those volunteering to take evacuees into their homes had pre-conceived ideas of London children being delinquent, dirty and unruly, who had never seen a cow or green fields and would not be able to cope with the culture shock, as they awaited the arrival of these 'dead-end kids' with some trepidation.

Additionally, a significant number of children, especially the girls, had long hair and were plagued with head lice, a problem exacerbated by the fact that evacuation had taken place during the school holidays and so they hadn't been checked by the school's 'nit nurse'. Some of the poorest evacuees, used to sharing their parents', or sibling's bed or, in some cases, sleeping under it, were confused when faced with new sleeping arrangements. One MP volunteered to put up ten evacuees in his large country home but received thirty-one. He wrote: 'I got a shock . . . I had little dreamt that English children

Evacuees setting of to the unknown, with a mixture of fear and excitement.

could be so completely ignorant of the simplest rules of hygiene and that they would regard the floors and carpets as somewhere to relieve themselves'. Some of the children were perplexed at being given a toothbrush and paste since they had never cleaned their teeth before and expressed surprise in their letters home on such matters as: hot water coming out of the tap, a lavatory being upstairs and carpets!

I remember clearly the night our small mixed group arrived at 'I-knew-not-where' (it turned out to be Portland in Dorset), first to a school hall to be 'welcomed' with a cup of cocoa and a piece of 'soda cake' then, regardless of family ties, the girls were separated from the boys. I cannot imagine now how those sisters parted from their brothers must have felt at that moment, but I do remember how upsetting it was for me as (against our mum's last orders to stay together) it split my cousin Joyce Galvin and I apart. Eventually

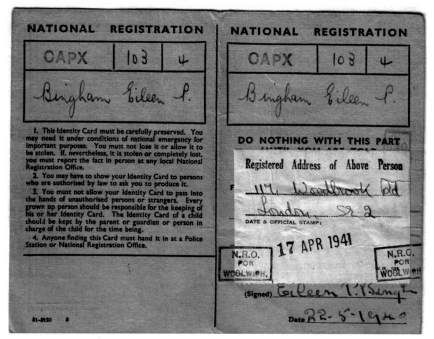

National Registration Identity Card for Eileen P. Bingham, later Mrs Charles Smith.

the two separate, bedraggled groups of girls and boys were marched to the 'collection point' outside the local bank to await selection, akin to a sort of 'human cattle market'.

At last, as darkness gathered and our pathetic little party diminished to just two – a classmate and myself. I choked back the tears as I realised just how alone I was. To this day, the personal abject loneliness of that time has never, thank God, been repeated.

Standing there with Andrew Monteith, a fatherless boy who had been in a sanatorium with TB (the dreaded disease of those days), we at last caught the eye of a very large man who had arrived a little late at the 'cattle market' when all the 'best ones' had gone. Before being allowed to depart, there was one final check: 'Have you both got a spare pair of underpants, pyjamas, vest, socks, toothbrush, comb, soap and flannel?' We wearily nodded assent but both knew that we didn't have toothbrushes or toothpaste. Eventually we were allowed to leave and to know our new guardian's name, as the billeting officer said, 'Right there boys, off you go with Mr Marsh and behave yourselves!' Mr Marsh gripped our trembling hands and took us to the end of the main street and along a dark lane to his humble home.

The Marsh house on that dark night could well have been the setting for a Brontë or Dickens novel, as it appeared eerily and completely isolated from the main street on the edge of 'nothingness', presenting a less than welcoming spectre. When day broke, that 'nothingness' turned out to be a massive quarry which appeared to start at the end of the garden and to go on forever. The detached house to which Mr Marsh took us both had obviously been built in the preceding century, with accommodation and toilet facilities to match its Victorian age, whilst its all-brick construction was in stark contrast to the rest of the closely packed stone cottages housing local quarry workers which typified the area.

Inside the house we were met by Mrs Marsh and her two sons who were about nine and twelve years old, who had been allowed to stay up to gasp and giggle at us poor, travel-weary wretches. Mr Marsh, who worked in the local Royal Naval Dockyard, was an ex-Royal Navy stoker who had served in the First World War and was what I would now describe as the strong silent type in the traditional 'head of family' way. In the short time that I stayed under his roof, I became aware of the absolute control he exercised over the dutiful Mrs Marsh and the three children (there was also a daughter, Lilly, of about fifteen or sixteen) which, including us, soon became five.

I admit to being scared of Mrs Marsh, both at first sight and sound, as she barked, 'Have you got your ration books and Identity Cards?' After fumbling in our belongings for them and handing them over for close scrutiny, Mrs M. said, 'I suppose you boys are tired and by the looks of yer need a good feed!' The kitchen-cum-dining room we were standing in was sparsely furnished with a large, scrubbed white-wood table and some rickety old chairs standing on a bare stone floor, but it was warmed by a massive fireplace, which Mr M. occasionally spat in, watching it sizzle on the burning embers before resuming sucking on his pipe. In the cold light of the next morning the house seemed nowhere as big as it did when it loomed out of the dark to fill my tired eyes the night before.

Andy and myself were given a very bare and cold attic room with a tiny window looking out over a large, deep quarry and, in the distance, the infamous Borstal Institution for young offenders. Our bed was an antique iron one with a flock filled mattress which felt and smelled cold and damp and had belonged to old Mrs M. who, the Marsh boys gleefully chided us, had died in it. She must have slept alone and been very large because as we clambered into the bed, so we both automatically rolled towards each other into the permanent centre depression.

The Portland schools had to be shared between the local children and the evacuees and this rather stretched the resources of some, to the extent that one group had lessons in the morning and the other group in the afternoon. The 'blank' periods were usually devoted to singing, music and sport, which most of my kind saw as 'play' rather than lessons.

There was a certain amount of mostly friendly bantering between the two sides, as we referred to the locals as 'country bumpkins' and they responded with 'townies' when referring to us. A particular sore point between us was the 'country bumpkins' accusing us 'townies' of running scared from the German bombers. Their taunts, unfortunately, backfired on them proving an immense embarrassment though it could have proved worse still, to the national authorities who, in their infinite wisdom, decided that the safest destination for the kids from London's docklands with its merchant ships, would be another dock area with its Royal Navy warships! The crazy logic of why Portland in Dorset was chosen remains a mystery. Whilst the authorities didn't notice the strategic value of Portland and its naval base, the Germans certainly did by attacking Portland Harbour well before they raided the London docklands and my home.

On a bright morning two days after being evacuated from the risk of air attacks on London, I was taken by my new foster parents to the local church, in Portland's Easton district. When the service had finished, we were all asked to wait in the church grounds for an important announcement at 11.00am. Whilst still bewildered by my unfamiliar surroundings and strangers and looking for my cousin Joyce and friend 'Munchie' McCall, the church bell started to ring and we were all told to be quiet as Neville Chamberlain made his now famous speech, announcing the declaration of war against Germany.

On 1st September, Hitler's troops had invaded Poland and by so doing, brought the British and the French, as guarantors of Polish safety, to declare war on Germany, at 11.00 am, Sunday, 3rd September.

As we left the church we were greeted by an air-raid siren wailing, soon to become a familiar sound, but leaving many of us unsure of whether it was a test or reality. However, our fears were soon quelled by the welcoming 'all clear' siren. We walked 'home' in almost complete silence, as perhaps the Marshes were contemplating what effect the war would have on them and their most recently acquired charges – Andy Monteith and myself.

That weekend saw an unprecedented rush to buy blackout material although this was mainly due to the penalties that would be enforced by the authorities, rather than out of a fear of the Luftwaffe at that stage of the war. The supplies of blinds: black calico or linen, blackout paint, cardboard, brown paper and drawing pins and tin-tacks soon ran out and replacement materials became almost unobtainable. Whilst some of the people welcomed the black-out (mostly those engaged in nefarious activities), the majority hated it as an infernal nuisance and a bigger menace to civilian lives than the conflict on the battlefields. In that first month of restrictions, the number of road accidents nearly trebled and even three months later, when people had begrudgingly adjusted to picking their way through the blacked-out streets and crossing the roads, there were over ten fatalities reported. In my home area, complacency started to creep in when the expected air attacks failed to materialise and though there was some easing of the restrictions on public lighting, total blackout rules were strictly enforced should the air-raid warning sound.

War – It's official!

Return from evacuation

To evacuee children like myself, brought up in the close-packed streets of Canning Town and Custom House, the choice of anywhere but the East End had to be right, and Portland fitted the bill. With its almost limitless play area, afforded by the quarries (famous for their Portland Stone), its Church Ope Cove beach, and without the restrictions normally afforded by caring parents it was perfect for us boys. The high risk from German air attack on the naval base paled into insignificance compared to the freedom we now found ourselves with.

That was, until the time I lost my best friend, Maurice 'Munchie' McCall, who was my childhood neighbour and school chum of the same age as myself.

One sunny day he went playing around the large quarry at the back of the house where I was billeted, slipped and fell into the depths and was crushed by a dislodged boulder. This finally persuaded my mother that 'enough was enough!' so, just five weeks later, driven by her view that, 'If you're going to die then it will be with me!', she brought my cousin Joyce and myself back home to Canning Town where, after enduring the hard winter of 1939–40, we survived the ensuing Blitz and spent the rest of the war there in the bomb-blasted but undefeated East End of London.

CHAPTER EIGHT

Bombed Out! – The Blitz Hits Home

At the outbreak of the war, my father was working on the 'Arundel Castle' as First Cook but, on returning to its home port, his ship was commandeered by the Royal Navy. It was promptly turned into an 'Armed Merchantman' operating in the convoys across the Atlantic, ferrying 'Lease-Lend' goods from America or in the Russian Arctic on the perilous convoys to Archangel and the hazardous Malta convoys in the Mediterranean at the mercy of the Luftwaffe bombers flying from bases in nearby Italy, whose Government had joined the Nazi war machine to form the Axis. My father was now an official member of the Royal Navy and was given the rank of Petty Officer, rising to Chief Petty Officer, before being invalided out of the Senior Service after someone dropped a 4-inch artillery shell onto his foot. This hurt him more psychologically than physically because it happened not in action, where he could have felt some sense of purpose for the German bombing about to be unleashed on his family back home in London, but in gunnery practice. After that mishap my father reverted to his former Merchant Navy role.

Through the summer of 1940 I saw the Battle of Britain acted out above me on a daily basis, in which Hitler tried unsuccessfully to destroy the Royal Air Force and achieve air supremacy by all out aerial attacks, night and day. London, particularly the docklands area of the East End and my home, suffered horrendously in the bombing, along with many other places. The full-scale air assault on the capital, the 'real Blitz', as it came to be called, started on the 7th September, when Hitler knew he was losing the opportunity to invade Britain. He switched his objective to paralysing London – the nerve centre of Allied resistance.

Every night for the following two months some two hundred German Dornier and Heinkel bombers raided the South East, headingmainly for London and the docks. They dropped not only high explosives (HE) but thousands of incendiary bombs. We were assured that if the incendiary bombs were discovered immediately they could be neutralised with domestic shovels, sand, a stirrup-pump and a bucket! Undetected, they became uncontrollable and set whole buildings ablaze. 'Fire watching' became an extra task for many weary Londoners who worked on a rota system of unpaid overtime at their place of employment.

Fear and tension was palpable as we saw our homes and our city exploding and burning all about us. But through it all, those who endured more than

400 air-raids that autumn displayed wonderful spirit which surprised even themselves. It was reported that one Sunday, just after Christmas, a particularly severe raid on the City just to the west of our home saw twenty-eight incendiaries fall on St Paul's. Through nothing short of a miracle, the cathedral was saved. Over sixty separate fires raged in the area. A journalist wrote, 'The dome seemed to ride the sea of fire like a great ship'. Pictures from that time showed the city streets carpeted in hosepipes and records detailed over 200 people were killed that one night. On the north side of the cathedral, some 63 acres were reduced to a waste of smouldering ashes and rubble. In subsequent raids that autumn another 100 or more acres were completely devastated and, of the City's tightly packed 460 acres, over 164 were reduced to ruin.

We adventurous boys collected the unexploded incendiary bombs, which were approximately 18 inches long by some 3 inches in diameter with a dark green tri-fin attached to their silver aluminium body and foolishly tried to dismantle them by banging them on the ground or throwing them from the upstairs rooms of bombed-out houses. Luckily, having failed to make them explode and burn, they were confiscated by the air-raid wardens. More usefully the containers that had housed the incendiary cluster were fashioned by some people into lamp standards, whilst the two-tone blue silk parachute fabric and cord were used for a variety of purposes about the home and the body.

Nowhere was the effect of the bombing more acute than in the East End, where the poor were rendered even poorer as they lost everything except their indomitable spirit. In the face of adversity, in a war which was not of our own making, people all around me clambered their way through devastation and destruction using unbreakable will and valiant strength as their guiding light.

The Blitz came early and real to me on the night of Friday, 6th September 1940, when a stray bomb killed our neighbour's eldest son, Jackie McCall. He stepped off the bus at the top of our road after work, was struck down and instantly killed. The next day, Saturday 7th September, became forever etched in Eastender's memories as Black Saturday. It was the start of the most intense phase of the Blitz. Much of the old East End – the wharfs and docks just south of us and where my grandfather had stepped off the ship from Australia some fifty years earlier – disappeared in a pall of thick black smoke with considerable loss of life. For the next fifty-six nights London was to be bombed from dusk until dawn and its intensity stepped up from mid-October, as German bombers droned up the silver line of the Thames to the biggest target in the world. The very river which had led the Romans to camp and name their English city 'Londinium', from which London developed, was now being used by the Luftwaffe to destroy it.

From then on it seemed the air-raid warning siren became routine, forcing my mother, sister and I to take up permanent, night-time residence in the air-raid shelter as the frightening after-dark attacks increased and systematically

7th September 1940, one of hundreds of Heinkel 111 bombers flies over the Thames to wreak destruction on the docklands of East London on 'Black Saturday'.

The scene from London Bridge on that fateful Saturday afternoon as the East End goes up in smoke.

Bomb damage on Friday, 6th September 1940, the eve of the Blitz on London. At South Molton Road, a Home Guard stands with his rifle to keep sightseers and possible looters away.

destroyed the area. During these continuous raids we had to rely on the mobile canteens, run by the WVS and the Salvation Army. We had no gas, water or electricity for much of the time on which to cook or make the essential morale boosting 'cuppa'.

The terraced house where we lived also became home to my grandparents, two uncles and the Galvin family, all of whom had been bombed out from further down the road by what was reputed to be the Capital's biggest bomb. The crater it left measured 120 feet across with a depth of 90 feet. It was terrible for my aged grandparents and cousins, moving into such a tightly packed space. We were packed like sardines. The house was already frontless so we used a hastily rigged tarpaulin to cover the bomb damage. The back windows had all been blasted out and were covered with heavyweight black-out material battened to the frames.

Without gas and electricity, smelly oil lamps burned indoors each day whilst burning bomb debris wood in the open grate kept us warm. A total blackout was in force, air-raids or not, and the unimaginable risk posed by using oil lamps and burning candles, plus the fact that torch batteries were almost unobtainable made it necessary for us all to get used to doing every-thing in complete darkness.

The blackout rules were strict and if someone saw even a chink of light from a window or doorway, the authorities would knock at the door if you had one and tell you forcibly to 'put it out!'. Night seemed to last for days and

Bomb damage on Friday, 6th September 1940, the eve of the Blitz on London. The morning after; nearby Cundy Road was on the Luftwaffe's flight path.

Bomb damage on Friday, 6th September 1940, the eve of the Blitz on London. Children come to look at the damage to a house in Mortlake Road.

ARP (Air Raid Precautions) members assess the bomb damage in Beckton Road, where our close neighbour, teenager Jackie McCall was killed on Friday, 6th September 1940, on the eve of the official start to the Blitz.

Beckton Road school 'blitzed' on the night of 18th September 1941. The architecture of this school was typical of so many other East End school buildings. At the start of the Blitz local schools were used as Rest Centres to care for the hundreds of people who had been bombed out of their homes in Canning Town and Custom House.

The Prime Minister, Mr Winston Churchill, visits a familiar scene of bomb devastation in an East End street, 1940.

we sat quietly in the velvety dark, listening to the continuous explosions outside and the pounding of our own hearts inside. We wondered where the next one would fall.

But there were humourous moments too, such as when one of our neighbours decided before we lost power that he had the answer to the light problem and painted his bulbs black. All he got for his trouble was ridicule from his family as they stumbled about in almost complete darkness, not to mention the smell of burning paint, whenever he put the light on.

Though the 7th September might have been Black Saturday generally for West Ham Borough, it was also the case for my beloved West Ham United FC, who were attempting through it all to maintain a sense of normality. The Hammers were being thrashed at Upton Park by their greatest rivals, Tottenham Hotspur, 4–1, before the sirens sounded and their game was abandoned. As the air attack intensified the lingering fans had to flee for their very lives.

In those days of almost continuous air-raids, the nightly routine of going to bed in the shelter or the dug-out, regardless of the siren sounding or not, would often prove to be the best way to get some sleep. People felt comparatively safe and hoped they would miss the obligatory disturbance from the Heinkel and Dornier bombers of the Luftwaffe, that droned menacingly overhead.

In the depth of winter, our outdoor air-raid shelter was like a refrigerator. As we breathed out, so it condensed on the cold metal sides and ran or dripped down the corrugations to soak into whatever covering we were wearing. In addition to blankets, eiderdowns and hand-crocheted woollen quilts, old heavy overcoats were ideal in the damp and cold shelters. However, pride still dictated that you never revealed to your neighbours that you were covered in bed by coats instead of quilts. Imagine the embarrassment of a mother when, after tucking her two kids in for the night, the neighbours could hear the plaintive shouts of, 'Mum, Florrie's pulling the quilt off me! And now she's gone and torn the sleeve off!'.

In the summer, the shelter was unbearably hot and stifling during the night. Three adults shared the space with two children in an area smaller than a modern double bed. This forced us to accept a head-to-toe, space saving, sleeping arrangement. Depending on the previous night's damage to the home and its electricity, gas and water supplies, we had breakfast which comprised mainly American SPAM and dried egg prepared in a number of different ways. Alternatively, we would be fed from the WVS and Salvation Army mobile canteens, before going through all the mayhem and destruction all about us, off to school for just five hours of lessons, taken mostly in an air-raid shelter. For a 'Bob' (5p) we got dinner in the Government sponsored local British Restaurant.

Invariably night raids would coincide with the cooking of the family's evening meal which many housewives considered their first priority, despite the alarm siren. They would only make a panic dash for the dug-out at the sound of the approaching bombers. One particular incident involved the woman next door-but-one. She had been part way through the evening's fry-up, when the distant thud of a bomb and the mournful drones of approaching German planes were heard. As she instinctively raced for the safety of the shelter, she stopped in her tracks and yelled to her husband, 'I've forgotten my false teeth', to which he was unsympathetically heard to retort, 'They're dropping bombs, not bleedin' steaks!'

If we were at school when there was a daylight raid, the lessons were post-poned as teachers herded us across the playground to a double-brick-thick surface shelter. It was dimly lit and always smelled and felt damp. Sometimes, before we could evacuate the ground floor classrooms the heavy anti-aircraft (ack-ack) guns nearby would suddenly open up with ear-splitting percussions and the large, jagged pieces of shrapnel that fell onto the playground would prevent us getting to the safety of the shelter. The only alternative was to sit on the floor of the cloakrooms or under our desks. We were encouraged to sing or play loud games to forget the noise and danger of the scene outside. During such times the teachers took the opportunity to give us gas-mask training and this proved to be quite entertaining as we learned to talk to each other in sign language with our gas-masks on. Condensation and the inevitable runny nose often made this difficult though.

Looking out from the shelter at night, the darkness was often brightened by flashes from exploding bombs or the reply from the anti-aircraft guns sited in our local park. Sometimes the sudden crack of the ack-ack would scare the hell out of us as mobile guns would open up in the street outside our house. These sounds would often be accompanied by the smaller calibre rapid-fire Bofors guns, or pom-poms as their sound suggested. Most of the bombs that fell on us were between 100 and 500 lb and exploded on impact. However, some never detonated and the area had to be cleared whilst they were made safe by the bravery of the Royal Engineers bomb disposal teams. In addition to the HE bombs and incendiary clusters, some oil bombs were dropped to set fire to a wider area. Whilst the HE bombs made large craters, their damaging blast was limited by their penetration, often deep into the earth, before detonation. The Luftwaffe also resorted to very large landmines attached to parachutes, which made shallow craters but exploded on impact and literally swept vast areas to destruction.

Unless one has personally experienced an aerial bombardment whilst cowering in a terror intensified by darkness, the written word just won't cover it. In retrospect I am thankful that as a youngster, from the age of eleven to fourteen years old, that youthfulness diluted the fear that I would have most certainly felt had I been an adult and more aware of the life and death consequences the German raids regularly presented. Many servicemen home on leave found the Blitz terrifying and most openly admitted to being frightened during the raids. They became lost and scared without the familiar protection they felt from having their own weapons to hand. I think it was generally accepted that most of those on 'active service' worried more about their bomb threatened families, than the enemy they confronted on the world's battlefronts.

Two sounds that are forever imprinted in my memory from those days are the sound of the siren that caused my heart to leap and the monotonous piston-

Two East End women, at the sharp end of the Blitz, emerge from their Anderson air-raid shelter which saved their lives after their two-up-and-two-down home had been destroyed.

Typical scenes of the 'morning after' Blitz destruction caused during a Luftwaffe night raid on homes and factories in the docklands area of East End London in the Autumn of 1940.

The irrepressible spirit of the London Front Line ladies is illustrated by them still managing to smile in defiance at the adversity inflicted upon them by Goering's Luftwaffe bombers.

engine throb of the Heinkels and Dornier bombers. This droning was only broken by the sounds of high explosive bombs falling with a spine chilling whine and culminating with a dull thud which made our air-raid shelter shudder. We were reassured that if you heard the bomb whistling down, it would miss you. It was the bombs you didn't hear that killed you. It was rumoured that the enemy put 'screamers' into the fins of their bombs to increase the fear of their intended victims. It certainly had the desired effect on us.

More irrepressible spirit . . .

Throughout September 1940, London and particularly the docks and the East End had taken a terrible hammering, but its sheer size, as well as the skill and bravery of the RAF, prevented the Germans from delivering that 'knockout' blow to the capital and in particular to civilian morale. London's docks, in spite of their size and importance to the whole nation, though heavily bombed, were only one complex among many. The food and essential raw materials being shipped into Britain via other ports, were lessening the impact of the German war machine so, in early October, the Luftwaffe switched their attacks to Southampton and Liverpool as well as Midlands and Northern industrial targets. In November, Coventry was hit particularly hard by some 450 bombers, killing over 550 civilians in one single night and whereas London's most famous buildings escaped complete demolition, in Coventry almost everything either went up in flames or was flattened.

As the raids on us eased, so we could take account of the terrible losses that our locality had suffered. We remembered with delayed shock the great loss of life when nearby Hallsville Road School in Canning Town received a direct hit on the night of the 10th September 1940. It was being used as a rest centre and a transit base for the bombed-out homeless prior to their evacuation to safety. So many women, children and elderly were killed, that the local funeral services and the East London Cemetery couldn't cope and many of the victims had to be interred where they lay in the ruins. It became to them, a permanent tomb, which today is marked with a commemorative plaque. The full horror of the tragedy was not readily known until relatives, friends and classmates never appeared. Some absences were accepted as having been evacuated according to the original schedule, on the afternoon and evening of the fateful night. Official estimates suggested seventy-three people had been killed.

Mass funerals and graves were common with so many unidentified bombing victims. In December 1940, seven firemen were killed when their station was hit and it was a sad occasion as we watched their coffins being borne on fire appliances as they made their way along Hermit Road to the cemetery. Two of the firemen had roads named after them in the post-war reconstruction of Canning Town.

While it seemed that the heat had been taken off London, the Germans reminded us that they hadn't finished with us by carrying out a massive incendiary raid on the City of London. On Sunday, 29th December 1940, a relatively small attack by about 150 aircraft started over 1,500 separate fires, of which about 90 per cent raged unchecked. The fire fighting problem was compounded by a Thames neap-tide, making it impossible for the fire hoses to reach down into the river and in 2 hours the fires, fanned by a strong westerly wind, consumed everything between Moorgate, Aldersgate Street, Cannon Street, and Old Street, producing the biggest area of war devastation in the whole of Britain.

As a child at the time, the local park was the only place of recreation. As in most wartime parks there were no swings or slides because what had not been commandeered for scrap to aid the war effort (as had our school and house railings) was left rusting into decay and danger through lack of local council money and manpower. However, such wartime deprivations could not stop us from having hours of childish fun on a seesaw, fashioned from an old bomb-damaged floorboard, precariously balanced on a disused oil drum along with other 'custom made' toys.

We didn't have a cinema since the local Odeon built in 1939 had been Blitzed beyond repair whilst the New Imperial (originally 'Relfs Music Hall' rebuilt in 1909 partly from materials from the former Imperial Theatre in Westminster) was always being closed for repair, safety reasons, shortages of heating fuel and staff. Our only under-cover meeting place was the local St Albans Church Hall. This was often taken over to provide temporary accommodation for victims of the Blitz (and again in 1944, when it was commandeered for troops of the Allied Expeditionary Force en-route through the docks, to the Normandy beaches on 'D' Day, 6th June 1944). The local swimming pool was closed down to be used as a Rest Centre for those made homeless by the bombing and, like the cinema, there wasn't any heating fuel or staff to manage it any way.

Most newspaper and confectionery shops, where the weekly ration was just two ounces of sweets if there were any, as well as almost all other non-essential shops, were closed either through bomb damage, lack of goods or the obvious hasty evacuation of their owners. Whilst indoors, daylight was shut out by battened-up windowless frames and there was only a one-band wireless for the daily war news and some light entertainment such as music, plays and variety. The popular comedy show of the time was *ITMA* (*It's That Man Again*) that man being Tommy Handley. The content of the show was, if anything, more popular than the sacred *Nine o'clock News*. Its characters were sur-realistically bizarre, yet they were possessed of an awful familiarity with their endless repetition of catchphrases, which became part of our everyday vocabulary. More people would have recognised a reference to Colonel Chinstrap, or the German spy, 'Funf', than the Chancellor of the Exchequer or the Chief of the Imperial General Staff.

Through the radio came the propaganda broadcasts from Nazi Germany by the infamous Lord Haw Haw, the soubriquet for a traitorous Englishman – William Joyce (hanged as a war criminal in 1945). It was compulsive listening causing every adult to tune in to hear the lies being told. It was rumoured that his outrageous confrontational style of broadcasting would rile his listeners so much that they would vent their anger on the radio by smashing it and so prevent them from tuning in to the BBC for the real truth about how the war was progressing, or not. One particular memory of Lord Haw Haw's out-pourings were, 'We're not going to drop bombs on the East End tonight, but flea powder on you poor rats as you crawl into your nightly homes'.

If the cinemas had been open we might have seen, albeit interrupted by enemy aircraft, the most popular wartime film, *Gone With The Wind*, which ran for about four years from 1940. The most popular song after the evacuation from Dunkirk and the fall of France which resulted in the dropping of

We're Going to Hang Out Our Washing on the Siegfreid Line, was *The White Cliffs of Dover* sung by the local girl made good from East Ham, Vera Lynn.

Before the 'Polo' (i.e. The Apollo Theatre) and the 'Addo' (Adamson Road Theatre) were finally demolished by the Luftwaffe, we would go up on a Saturday morning for the kids 'tuppenny rush' to see The Three Stooges, with Will Hay and Moore Marriot, the Marx Brothers, Charlie Chaplin, plus many other third-rate silent movies. All suffered from poor projection and film quality, but as we didn't know any better it did nothing to spoil our enjoyment and rendered us all oblivious to the drab and decaying surroundings of the flea pit cinemas. 'Bunking in' at the wartime cinema was considered fair game to prevent paying but an even better ruse was to play on the local park's putting green, as tickets for that were identical, in nearly all respects, to the cinema tickets and easily fooled the usherettes in the dark.

Our un-chaperoned naughtiness in the cinemas was restricted to either pulling hair of the girl in front or standing on the top of the back row seat, immediately below the projection opening and using our hands to create shadow silhouettes on the screen in the projection beam. It was amazing how many animal shapes could be made, but the real hilarity was caused when a finger and thumb appeared to pull the hair, or pick the nose, of the on-screen image before you were caught and thrown out. The best cinema was The Grand, nicknamed the 'Haymarket', not after its famous West End counterpart, but because of the horse-feed depot next door! It was a slightly up-market attraction, compared to the two Custom House cinemas, so it was referred to as a 'bug hutch' rather than the lower term 'flea pit' and 'bunking in' was almost impossible because of the overpowering Commissionaire who had seemingly forgotten that he had left the Army in 1918.

Local schools encouraged football and cricket be actively played, albeit that there was a shortage of grass pitches and those that were available deteriorated through lack of care and bomb damage. Even our street 'kickabouts' were no longer possible, as the roads became bomb-cratered, pot-holed and strewn with bomb debris. Somehow, games were organised on a weekly inter-schools basis and the prized 'Sun Shield' competition was run on a knock-out system where teams representing adjacent Boroughs were pitted against each other with intense rivalry and passion.

By 1941 my grandfather and grandmother had moved to a more spacious home in Canning Town's South Molton Road but they hadn't been there long when it was completely destroyed in the Blitz. This was just another example of so much collateral damage from the bombing of London's docks. This forced them to move up to the other end of the road. Though bomb-damaged, this house was just about habitable. They remained there until the early 1950s, until the Council completed the long-awaited slum clearance which the German Luftwaffe had started and new housing sprang from the ruins.

In early 1941, eight air-raid wardens were killed by a direct hit on their Wardens Post in nearby Custom House School. But we of the East End became evem more united by our grief. Sometimes it would be days, or even weeks, before bomb victims were found in the rubble of their homes, unless they had been reported missing to the Air Raid Wardens. After one particularly bad raid my grandmother told me next morning to go and see if her friends Mr and Mrs Raven, who lived a couple of streets away, were alright. When I got there I found the house demolished and, as I stood gawping, the rescue team unearthed them both, dead, from beneath the kitchen table. My gran could barely believe me when I told her the sad news.

The final phase of the London Blitz began in mid-April 1941, with a raid by 685 planes and ended with a more savage attack on the night of 10th/11th May, when over 700 tons of bombs and incendiaries were dropped. This killed 1,436 people and the next morning a third of London's streets were impassable, without gas, water or electricity.

By late spring of 1941, Goering's Blitz had almost reached a point of stale-mate, mainly due to the significant improvement of the British air defences by the arrival of radar-equipped-ground directed night fighters and the increase in the production of new fighter aircraft. As the RAF triumphed in the Battle of Britain, Hitler was forced to switch his attention elsewhere. He directed them particularly at Russia, so our air-raids lessened between 1941 and 1943. However, for me it still meant school hours were restricted for safety reasons to between 10 am and 3 pm, as it was uncertain when the raiders might return. This slackening of the German attacks meant our houses could be patched up to a higher standard than our initial emergency repair efforts, so making them somewhat more habitable. The majority of repairable war damage was caused by the blast from nearby bombs, mostly resulting in fallen ceilings and broken windows. For these there appeared to be only two materials – asbestos sheet and tarred felt. It was surprising how many new backyard sheds began to appear!

CHAPTER NINE

Starved Out! – Austere Times; Resourceful Eastenders

As we emerged battered but unbroken by what the Luftwaffe had thrown at us, we soon came to know the strangling effects of the German U-Boat 'Wolf Packs' attacking our lifeline convoys far out in the Atlantic where my father was serving, as the enemy moved on to trying to starve us out.

Rationing

One wartime etiquette that remains with us to this day, is the obligatory queue – everybody queued for almost everything; for transport, ration books and food. But in those days when the front of the queue had been reached there was often little or nothing to be had. Even if there was just a couple of people standing outside a butchers or grocers, people would assume it was queue for something and so would join it expectantly. As mischievous schoolboys, we often used this to play practical jokes on our neighbours. Two or three of us would stand in a line outside a sweet shop in a mock queue and within minutes, it would grow to a point where we would be able to quietly slink away leaving more gullible people to wonder why or what, they were queuing for.

Shortages and rationing were inconveniences which officially applied to everyone and provided a six year daily scenario of ration books, endless queues, utility clothes and house wares and the introduction of dubious substitutes such as whale-meat and dried egg. The automatic response to every complaint that arose from these restrictions was, 'There's a war on, you know!'.

Although a ration scheme had been prepared as early as 1938, ready for implementation in September 1939, it only became effective in January the following year. The first foodstuffs to be rationed were sugar (8 oz), butter (8 oz), ham and bacon (4 oz). In March meat was rationed, by price rather than by weight, with each person over the age of six, entitled to 1s 10d (9p) of meat per week. Though offal was not rationed, it was almost unobtainable, unless you befriended the local butcher. July saw the introduction of tea rationing, clearly an indication of a worsening situation for the country at war. Heavy merchant shipping losses (well over 2,000 in the war) mostly in the Atlantic to German 'U' boats, posed a serious threat to our food supplies and, although I did not comprehend it at the time, to our family's security, as my father was serving on North Atlantic convoy duties. This deteriorating situation was to be made worse by the Japanese invasions in the Pacific which cut off vital sources of rice, sugar and tea.

Next on the ration list were preserves, sweets (8oz) and cooking fat (8oz, of which 4oz had to be margarine). In May 1941, cheese was rationed to a miserly 1oz per week and followed, a month later, by shell eggs as in real not powdered eggs, based on controlled distribution which amounted to each adult getting about thirty eggs a year. A points system was applied to canned meat, fish, and vegetables etc., which enabled the customer to choose between a range of tinned goods, each with a fixed points price. This system was extended, in January 1942, to dried fruit, rice and tapioca. The following month canned fruit, tomatoes and peas were added to the list and in April, it was the turn of condensed milk and breakfast cereals. Before the year's end, syrup, treacle, biscuits, oat flakes and rolled oats were on ration too, adding to the discomfort of the 'Home Front'.

As a result of the effects of the U-Boats combined with other setbacks for the Allies in North Africa, the Mediterranean & SE Asia theatres of war, further rationing hit us on the 'Home Front' hard. In August 1942 the adult meat ration was reduced to 1s 2d (7p) per week and included beef, veal, mutton, and pork, but not rabbit or poultry. This was equivalent to about a pound of meat per person per week. Rationing produced a monotonous diet but one that was shared as equitably and efficiently as possible across the nation. There were however, winners and losers as those living alone fared less well than large families who could pool their rations and make the most of what was available.

Shortages of pretty much everything led to a rampant alternative economy, the highly illegal 'black market'. Better known today as 'wheeling and dealing', many people in those days literally only managed to live on what they could scrounge or barter or steal. Mrs Neal was a big, rough tough woman neighbour of ours. She worked in the nearby Tate & Lyle's sugar factory at Silvertown near the docks. With her large rotund body, she became expert at smuggling sugar out of the factory to sell, or exchange for other scarce or rationed treats on the black market. Grannie would supplement our meagre sugar ration by dealing with Mrs Neal, for which we and particularly I as a young child was grateful. This went on for a long time before grannie was told that, 'Mrs Neal nicks the sugar and brings it out in her bloomers'! Mrs Neal's long bloomers or 'passion killers' appeared to me as a young boy the size of the Army's bell tents. I had seen these XL drawers hanging on the clothes-line for days in all weathers only being brought in when she needed to change her underwear, or restock our sugar! Imagine my horror to think of all that loose sugar contained in the confines of Mrs Neal's 'XL' drawers. I avoided sugar, despite my youthful sweet tooth, for many years afterwards!

Just along the road from Tate & Lyle was John Knight's soap factory. It was a stinking place, the soap being made of unimaginable 'ingredients' such as animal bones! Mr Tucker another of our neighbours, worked there. There was no soap powder then and washing was done using potato-crisp-like white soap-flakes. Mr Tucker, was our soap smuggler. Mrs Tucker would stash the smuggled flakes in a sort of mattress cover under the bed clothes in their house. This however had to be abandoned as poor old Mr Tucker became incontinent, wetting the bed so often as to make the selling of the smuggled soap too problematical. I was happy however, on two counts. It saved me another of my 'sworn to secrecy' weekly errands, going to the Tuckers with an old sweet jar which they filled for 'tuppence', less than today's penny. It also helped maintain or possibly encourage my reluctance to wash!

Wartime flour was brownish and coarse. Producers kept the wheatgerm in for health and labour-saving reasons. Another neighbour, Jack Galvin, worked at the Spillers Flour Mill at Silvertown. Without the benefit of Mrs Neal's bloomers smuggling flour out of this factory was just too difficult for Jack to conceal. But Jack was not to be beaten and there were many desperate for additional rations. Jack would walk home with his big black leather work boots filled with unmilled corn. It must have been agony for him, the hard corn pressing into and chaffing his feet over the 2 mile journey home. My uncle Frank an engineer at the Plessey factory in nearby Ilford which made aircraft parts and engines devised an ingenious system to get the smuggled brown flour back to pre-war whiteness, making it more palatable. He designed and built a mechanical silk-screen rotating sieve which he kept hidden in the upstairs of the house. This gave us finer whiter flour by separating out the coarser brown grains and husks to feed the chickens that were kept also illegally in many a back-yard of the East End. One couldn't be too fussy in those days about the source of the weekly shopping! Nowadays, during the weekly visit to the supermarket I can't help but to think back to the wartime days of rationing when choice was not an option. I recall the complete absence of any tropical fruit, especially oranges and bananas. It must have been about three or four years between my last wartime orange and the next, when my father brought some home from one of his seagoing travels and my mother gave me a whole one all to myself, with a warning to, 'eat it slowly, because you might not get another one for years'. Seeing my futile attempts to peel the thick skin, she took the orange from me and cut it into quarters so that I could get more readily to the orange flesh, belatedly satisfying the mouth-watering impatience of being without oranges for about a third of my young life. I don't think I shall ever forget that stirring of my taste buds. My mother was right; I didn't see another orange for years!

A sample of some wartime posters

Left: A famous cartoon by the Daily Mirror's Philip Zec, published in March 1942. It enraged the government, which took it to mean that seamen were risking their lives for profiteers at home, and the Mirror was briefly threatened with suppression before the row blew over.

A sample of some wartime books.

Butter was always a rare treat on a Sunday in the Maudesley and Smith households where 'marge' usually reigned supreme. For many of my childhood years, jam or any other spread was onto dry bread except when visitors came, then to prevent the jam soaking into the bread, a thin spread of 'marge' was allowed but never butter, because 'That was a waste!' Imagine my gran's and mother's rage when, during the cold winter of 1942, I was given the job of holding the almost solid butter ration in front of the open grate for it to melt a little, but in my disinterest allowed the precious butter to slide off the dish and into the fire causing it to burn fiercely – but not as fiercely as my face and bare arms did as mum laid into me. Another notable 'bashing' was also ration-related when I was sent for potatoes and paraffin for our wartime oil lamps and 'Primus' cooking stove. The paraffin was put into a quart beer bottle which had a screw stopper that hadn't been tightened, with the result that with both items in the same bag, the oil spilled over the potatoes completely ruining them as well as wasting the precious oil. Such was mother's anger that she wrestled me to the ground before my grandfather came to my rescue. There was no Social Services or Government regulations in place in those days to protect you from a good 'wallop' at home, school, or just generally!

Probably the most common snack of the wartime East End was thickly sliced toast with whatever spread was available but if there was none, dunking in tea was the alternative. 'Dunking' became almost a national trait and one I have carried with me (and passed on to my son!) ever since. Our cookers did not have grills, neither were there toasters in working class homes, so toasting was achieved by sitting in front of an open fire with a long handled toasting fork – a slow chore. The length of time sitting so close to the fire would cause the female 'toasters' to be identified by a multitude of red rings formed beneath the skin of their bare legs, which caused us kids to tauntingly sing out, 'Ring-a-ring-a-roses', itself a reference to the 'Great Plague', some 300 years earlier.

One food that never seemed to be in short supply was the Cockney's staple diet – eels. Mainly they were of the jellied variety and usually sold in local street markets, particularly Petticoat Lane. This was the location of the famous Tubby Isaac's seafood stall that specialised in jellied eels but also did a roaring trade in cockles, whelks, winkles and shrimps. In the Queens Road market, near to the Upton Park football ground of West Ham United, there was always a thriving fishmonger's stall called 'Thakes of Barking Road' and I could never pass quickly by it as I stood fascinated, if not entirely mesmerised, by the three big shiny deep sided metal trays, each holding a squirming mass of live eels. Though every doomed creature looked alike to me, the trays were mysteriously marked '1/0*d*, 1/6*d*, and 2/6*d* per pound'. Such pricing for the same weight of what appeared to be similar quality fish has remained a mystery ever since. This doubt was increased by personally witnessing eels from one tray slithering up and over into the next without old man Thake seeming bothered, even to the extent when on one Saturday market day another bystander of advancing years stood alongside me gazing at the trays before thrusting out a lightning arm to grab a large specimen and, in one obviously practised movement, stuff the unfortunate eel into a low down inside pocket of his shabby old raincoat!

The Government initiated a 'Dig for Victory' campaign. More and more gardens and back yards were cultivated and allotments created to produce vegetables whilst many installed chicken coops in their back yards. The rearing of chickens, mostly for their egg laying rather than for the table by these domestic hen keepers, was reckoned in 1944 to be producing about a quarter of the nation's supply of fresh eggs. Pig keeping, where space and neighbourly agreement was available, became another aspect of wartime animal husbandry. These non-farm-trained pig keepers mostly fed their charges on kitchen waste collected from designated waste-food bins distributed around the streets in most neighbourhoods. The wartime East End of London saw a return almost to the 'Dark Ages' with animals and humans being once again packed closely together.

It seemed impossible that during an all-out global war, which was being waged from the air destroying factories, food processing depots and farms, as well as from the sea where the German 'U' boats were blockading imports of food and other essentials, that the nation was assured by the authorities to be better nourished than it had been in the 1930s! Milk and vegetable consumption was up by about 30 per cent while meat consumption was in decline by 20 per cent. The emphasis of the Government report was obviously on nutritional content, rather than variety! That we survived the rationing was due not only to the average East Ender's traditional ability to exist on the minimum, but also to the United States who, through their Lease Lend agreement, met almost one-third of our food requirements at the height of the war. Besides thousands of cans of fruit, vegetables and evaporated milk plus fresh fruit, the Americans also introduced us to SPAM and dried egg, which made a good substitute breakfast.

There was a great wartime increase in communal eating, which partly compensated for the limitations of rationing. This was evidenced by the number of industrial factory canteens which rose from around 1,500 in 1939 to some 18,500 in 1944. Health experts of the day told us that moderately active adults needed about 3,000 calories a day whilst those engaged in heavy manual work needed much more. In view of this recommended calorie requirement, work canteens received an extra allowance of higher protein foods (meat, cheese, butter and sugar) which did much to close the calorie gap between the national average and those engaged on much heavier manual work. Work was never so popular in the East End as during the war years!

The Government also opened up a string of subsidised 'British Restaurants', run by local authorities. By September 1943 there were over 2,000 such restaurants serving some 600,000 meals a day at about 1s (5p) a head. The labour-saving, self-service style of these establishments was quickly copied by commercial caterers and carried forward to today, but this way of 'eating out' was then an entirely new experience for thousands of us in the East End. Poorer people who had never been into a restaurant in their lives and many not even into one of the worker's cafes dotted about the back streets near the docks and factories. There was a general feeling of a divide between the working classes and upper classes over eating out. Those with money and contacts could continue to dine out in pre-war style without the need of ration books. It was some comfort to me as a boy at the time when my gran said,

'I'd sooner 'av bread and drippin' than "horses doovers" (hors d'oeuvres) that lot eat.'

However self-indulgent the upper classes were, in the midst of the sacrifices being made by the East End working class, the poor were never envious of them eating their delicacies and enjoying their luxuries. Of far greater importance and satisfaction to the poorest East Enders was the fact that their kids were now getting free school milk and dinners – a major social advance.

Clothes rationing was introduced in June 1941 and was again based on a points system where sixty-six points were intended to provide one complete outfit a year. However, in the following spring, the points were reduced to sixty (or seventy for manual workers for their overalls etc.) over a fifteen-month period. This ration did not go far, enabling a man to buy; one pair of shoes every eight months, one pair of socks every four months, one shirt every twenty months, one vest and pants every two years, one pair of trousers and one jacket every two years, one waistcoat every five years and one overcoat every seven years. This division of points to buy essential clothing left just three coupons (points) for items like handkerchiefs or the traditional must-have cloth cap.

Once again, like the rationing of foodstuffs, the well-off benefited from the points rationing of clothes as not only did they have well stocked wardrobes to start with, they could make modest additions of good quality gear, which cost the same as the shoddily made, inferior quality garments which clothed the poor. Most of us in the East End didn't even have a wardrobe; there were never enough clothes to put in one! My own 'wardrobe' consisted of two rusty nails banged into the back of my bedroom door; even these were odd sized. My 'best' shoes were wrapped in newspaper so that the family valuables and insurance policies could be kept together in my shoe box for safety.

Thanks to overseas aid arriving in wartime 'Bundles for Britain' from America and Canada, children around the streets of my home would often be seen in ill-fitting Western-style clothes, incongruously wearing heavy-weight Lumberjack's coats and fur hats complete with earmuffs even in the height of mid-wartime summers.

In May 1942 the Board of Trade implemented a number of restrictions, aimed at saving yet more material, to the manufacture of all men's and youth's jackets, waistcoats and trousers. These included; no double-breasted jackets, no more than three pockets, no slits, buttons on cuffs, not more than three front buttons, no patch pockets, half belt, fancy belt and no metal or leather buttons. Waistcoats had to be plain, single-breasted only, with no more than two pockets and five buttons, no back strap or chain hole. Trousers had to be of a maximum width of nineteen inches, with plain bottoms, no permanent turn-ups, no more than three pockets, no side or back straps, no extension to the waistbands and no pleats or elastic in waistbands. Plain most definitely was the order of the day; or else it was just plain nothing!

The same principle of cutting out unnecessary frills was applied to the so called 'Utility' clothes, introduced in 1942. These were rigorously controlled in both price and material. They were sold to us as a 'fashion revolution' by a leading female journalist, who went on to assure her readers that these new 'Utility' clothes at government controlled prices were excellent value, that they cut out unnecessary luxury and defeated the profiteer. Eventually 'Utility' clothing accounted for about 80 per cent of all production, and we all looked very plain indeed, some fifty years before 'minimalist' became chic.

From July 1940, the supply of timber for domestic use was cut off and only small quantities released to meet the needs of bombed-out families. By 1942, the shortage of new furniture was so acute it caused the Government to limit most of its manufacture to essential items only, each with a prescribed timber content of two qualities and three designs. The austerity theme was evident in 'Utility' furniture with its square, basic design but it served its purpose by making aesthetic virtue out of necessity and enabled newly-weds to at least acquire the very basic furnishings for their home.

The 'Utility' concept was eventually extended to cover a wide range of civilian requirements and became in the process, a consumer trading standard like the British Standards Kite mark of today. This ever widening 'Utility' policy embraced such items as crockery, linoleum, sheets, blankets, mattresses, pencils, domestic electrical appliances, sports gear, and even included jewellery.

One of the raw materials that the British industry relied almost fully upon was coal. All the pits in those wartime days were privately owned but their output suffered because of years of neglect, under-investment, labour shortages and the Government's hesitance over nationalising the industry. In 1943 the Government directed a proportion of the young men called-up for National Service into the mines but only about 15,000 of these 'Bevin Boys', drafted by this unpopular measure, served at the coal face. Reliance was placed on voluntary rationing by the public to save coal. Certainly it had already become a luxury in the homes of the East End.

During the war and before the introduction of the National Health Service in the post-war years, doctors were few and far between and a visit had to be paid for whilst prescription medicines were charged at the actual cost. For those in the area who were unable or unwilling to pay for treatment, there was always 'nature's cure'. For example children with whooping cough were taken for walks along the sewer bank towards the Beckton Gasworks, so that they could breathe in the supposedly beneficial tar vapours from the factory! For 'opening medicine' long, hard and thick liquorice sticks were given to children to chew at endlessly, being then told to lie on a horsehair pillow to 'breathe in the smell'.

I often saw other children suffering from malnutrition. They would be insensetively called out in front of the class, or taken outside in the hall, where the teacher dipped a big spoon into a jar of cod liver oil and malt and then held the poor child's head whilst administering it. The more fortunate of us, not having to get this dreaded spoonful would watch the 'victims' return to their seats with shudders and contorted facial expressions. Before the advent of the Welfare Service of the DSS, there was no child allowance, so to preclude any children being put at risk when the family breadwinner was ill or un-employed, one had to go to the Relieving Officer (RO) who would often subject applicants to a rigorous and degrading means test before giving them a food voucher.

However, all these terrible national shortages brought out the best in the British (particularly the women) as they turned their attention to 'make-do-and-mend' in their wartime drive to self-sufficiency. The old saying, 'Necessity is the Mother of Invention' saw the ladies dye paint or 'line' their legs when stockings were no longer available. Unfortunately its application could be difficult (especially the 'lining' of a straight seam up the back of the legs) and some leg-paint had a tendency to change colour during the day. Women improvised to ensure their continuing attractiveness by using bi-carbonate of soda dusted under their arms as an anti-perspirant, a mixture of olive oil and grated bees-wax as a skin softener, burnt cork as eyelash mascara, hair colour rinses from Reckitt's Blue and hair dressing lotion for both sexes from liquid paraffin. Some unscrupulous people in the workplace peddled cut-price cosmetics, like face powder home-made from a concoction of chalk dust and cheap scent and lipstick which, it was discovered, was found to contain a high admixture of lead, making it a danger to health. If the ladies needed it then there was always a substitute product available as almost every-one 'knew a man' who could put them in the way of scarce consumer goods.

Whilst all the basic food items were strictly rationed, the people of that time always seemed to come up with a meal, miraculously conjured out of nothing, and so we didn't actually starve. This did'nt stop some 'wag' with humour typical of the people of the day altering a notice in my local park from 'Keep Off The Grass' to 'Do Not Eat The Grass!'

CHAPTER TEN

Terror Returns – Doodlebugs Hit the Streets

As the war raged all around us, people discovered with amazement that, despite the almost continuous bombing, life was bearable and the war became the background to our everyday life. In particular, people had to become used to the smell and dirt, from plaster, pulverised brick and dust that hung interminably in the air and remained undisturbed for years in corners and crevices. Tons of soot, which had collected in the flues since the houses were built in the late eighteenth century, were literally 'sucked out' of chimneys by the vacuum, which followed the first bomb-blast wave. These smells did as much to remind us of the Germans air assaults as the sight of demolished homes and the piles of bomb debris which were an everyday part of our lives.

My last days at school

I finished my elementary schooling in the summer of 1942, when I left Russell Road School, where I had started on my fourth birthday what at that time appeared to have been a lifetime before in 1933. My final parting was not caused by the obvious bomb damage of enemy action, expulsion or any reason outside my mother or teacher's control, other than that I had been temporarily gifted a rare show of brilliance by winning a wartime scholarship to West Ham Municipal College in Romford Road, Stratford.

The fragmented eight-odd years which I spent in the classroom, or the school's shelter, receiving my elementary education in the three Rs (reading, 'riting and 'rithmetic) still provides me with many memories. Memories of the school's size and demise (post-war redevelopment), its grand architecture, its lofty, aloof and cold classrooms and its frightening aura radiating that Dickensian message – 'Abandon Hope All Ye Who Enter Here!' – with its gloweringly stern Headmaster, Mr Harding, who used to peer over the top of his pince-nez specs and twisting his steel-grey waxed moustache with one hand, whilst with the other, threateningly slapping the side of his leg with his punishment cane.

Though we all walked in fear of the headmaster (and to be sent to him by a teacher for any misdemeanour could bring on a premature brown-trouser attack), in the wartime circumstances it was a good basic education. But of lasting memory from that school was the fierce patriotism and pride therein, demonstrated by the frightening Mr Harding, as he would use his punishment cane with the arrogance of the archetypal Colonial, to point out on the class-room's large map of the world that the widely distributed red areas were the same colour as Great Britain (emphasising the 'GREAT'), then declare that 'We' owned a quarter of the world's land area; 'We' were the richest country in the world before the war and 'We' are sixty times the size of France, eighty-seven times the size of Germany and over four times the size of the USA! He would then leave with a satisfied smile.

I started at the college in 1942 where, with unbelievable foresight, the local Education Authority, recognising that the tide of war was turning way before any of us did and with an eye on the post-war rebuilding of the war-ravaged Borough, opened the West Ham School of Building and Architecture. I was one of the inaugural intake where I learned the basic skills of drawing and building that were to stand me in good stead in my later working and married DIY life.

My first days at work

In the summer of 1943 I was becoming restless with school life and started to 'feel out of it' as my friends from the old elementary school had, or like me were reaching, their fourteenth birthdays and were allowed to leave school to go to work. Work meant more money in the pocket than I was getting as a schoolboy and jobs beckoned in those labour-short times at local factories such as Tate & Lyle, Ford's and the Docks etc, where a fourteen year-old could earn about thirty bob a week (£1.50). I pestered my poor mother for the whole of the summer holidays to let me leave, even threatening to run away if she didn't, until she relented and I left the college in 1943, four weeks before my fourteenth birthday, to 'go to work'.

I started work on 20th September 1943, thanks to our lady lay preacher at St Albans Mission Church who arranged an interview for me with the West Ham Electricity Department. I was taken on at West Ham Generating Station in the former slum and bomb-blasted area of Bidder Street, Canning Town, starting in the Stores as a trainee at the princely sum of fifteen shillings a week (75 pence). The taking of a 'cissy' job like that definitely bucked the local trend of higher paid 'real man's work' in the Docks, or at Ford's in Dagenham, my slight build already having stopped me going for a career in another locally popular profession – a boxer.

I was just four feet eleven inches tall and weighed about six stones, being considered 'tiny' for my age. I was put in the care of the Storekeeper, George Spraggins – a slight deformed figure of a man with a large humped-back, of which cruel jibes were made. My job was simple stock control, i.e. yesterday's stock minus today's issue and initiate re-ordering when necessary. On a boring scale of one to ten, this chore rated eleven and I couldn't wait to get out into the workshops for my promised engineering training.

After a couple of years with George and inhaling enough of his pipe-smoke to last me the next ten years and 'doing the rounds' of the workshops, I was upgraded to a General Office Clerk, which was more a general office dogsbody and included being a cyclist messenger, but at half a crown (12 ½ pence) a week better off. Whilst doing this job I was befriended by a man (Eric Smith) in the Drawing Office, who was about seventeen years my senior. He told me that I was wasting my time as a Clerk and he managed to get me into the Construction Engineer's Office as a Junior Draughtsman. Though being hopeless at mechanical drawing and testing Eric's patience to the full, I finally justified his faith in me, becoming a Chartered Mechanical Engineer later in life.

When however, as a naïve fourteen year old I had opted to join the ranks of working men rather than spend a further two financially unproductive years at school, the paltry sum of fifteen shillings (75 pence today) for a forty hour week, then represented a fortune, giving me almost total monetary independence, except of course for clothing, food and all those other things which my mother provided me for free. However, whether my switch from schoolboy to workman increased my engineering knowledge more than that about the facts of life, it is not for me to judge. What I, personally, remember from those career-forming days was the shock realisation that I was being stripped of my churchgoing and choirboy innocence and thrown headlong into the proverbial 'Den of Iniquity'.

I am not sure if the journey through those early teenage years (fourteen to fifteen) in which I experienced the awakening of my sexuality, was by way of nature taking its natural course, or if it was prematurely aroused by my automatic membership of the apprentices' 'dirty little buggers group'. What I am certain about, however, is although at the bottom of the learning curve of sexual knowledge and with absolutely nil experience, my up to then dormant masculine hormones began to activate and were filling me with increasing curiosity and attraction about and to the opposite sex, which in those day we referred to as 'Judies'.

In contrast to the sexual freedom of today, back in the 1940s the subject appeared to be 'Strictly Confidential – Adults Only!' which, with the strict controls governing the publishing business, the absence of any kind of illustrated titillating book (except 'Naturist' magazine depicting nude sun-worshippers but with their private parts obscured) dictated that one's knowledge was based mainly on hearsay. So, with seemingly every girl wanting to remain a virgin until married, the gaining of practical experience was nigh-on-impossible and curiosity unsatisfied. But our youthful frustration (education-ally, that is, not the practical) had to be assuaged by visits to our local 'bug hutch' theatre staging third-rate turns (as they were known) of mostly 'has-beens', or those girls seeking an escape from war work or call-up and who were making their stage debuts in the hope of getting one foot on the stairway to the 'big time'. Shows with female nudes were controlled by the Lord Chancellor's Office, who decreed that the artistes had to remain 'Statuesque' whilst onstage and discreetly placed hands or feather fans had to obscure private parts. Therefore, sex (or our code-name 'IT') continued to remain a mystery that fuelled the imagination of us younger apprentices and produced endless discussion at our tea-breaks.

It was at one of these 'IT' discussions, mainly consisting of boastful lies of successful sexual conquests, that I was overheard by the Workshop Foreman, who called me into his office to administer a salutary warning, as well as permanently imprinting on my mind, never to 'Kiss and Tell'. For that reason I have omitted from this book of my life, any reference to the 'ladies in my life'. Such an intentional omission does, of course, preclude the possibility of my wife belatedly suing me for divorce over my deceit in being economical with the truth. A secondary concern is that my son, reading that his father had once done (all those years ago) exactly what he was doing now, would have confirmed to him what his mother had always opinioned – 'So that's who I inherited it from?'

In the season of 1943–44 I started my teenage love affair with West Ham United FC. The Club derived it's nickname 'The Hammers', from the sledge-hammers used for riveting plates in the old Thames Ironworks, where the club began in 1895 playing its football. The team often had guest players from other professional clubs or members of HM forces stationed near to the 'Hammers' home. Due to the war and its associated difficulties for travel, Clubs were segregated into North and South regions and could select their opponents. First and Second Division sides however, were expected to play at least two Third Division clubs and the whole season's programme was more for entertainment and morale boosting thus demonstrating that, despite war, life was running a 'normal' course. West Ham won the 1940 Wartime Cup Final at Wembley, beating Blackburn Rovers one goal to nil. My heroes of those wartime teams were Archie Macaulay, Charlie Bicknell, Len Goulden, Ted Fenton, Harry Medhurst and the Walker and Corbett brothers.

My first match at Upton Park, named after a small village which once existed there, the home of 'The Hammers' was in September 1943. The match was played and well attended, despite the best efforts of the Luftwaffe, who were busy bombing the docks nearby! There was barely a wrinkly-tin or asbestos sheet left on the roof of the main stand and many nearby buildings had been completely destroyed in the bombing. The main viewing position at Upton Park in those days was a large earthen bank at one end, which became the famed North Bank in the post-war reconstruction of the club.

Those of us who had lived through the earliest and perhaps darkest war days, could never foresee Britain in 1943 'turning the tables' on Hitler's formidable Wehrmacht and Luftwaffe superiority. Most of the East End, particularly around the docks, was flattened – homes, offices, shops and factories gone; reduced to rubble, and the ultimate adventure playground for us kids of the war years. Following the Japanese bombing of Pearl Harbour on 7th December 1941, America had become involved in 'our' war and Britain was effectively no longer left standing alone in Europe. After three more years together we fought our way back from the brink.

Finally, by spring 1944 there was real hope in the air. The East End, as in many other locations around southern England, was alive for weeks with the assembly of men, vehicles and supplies in that spring. Our schools and church halls were taken over by troops from far off places I'd never heard of, with badges and buttons from the troops being the prized possessions of my school friends and I.

Tuesday 6th June 1944 was the most momentous of days and proved to be the turning point of the Second World War in the West. As dawn broke, our Allied forces waded ashore from seas onto the gun-raked beaches of Normandy. This was 'D-Day', the beginning of Operation Overlord, the greatest amphibious wartime manoeuvre the world had ever seen. Surprisingly, the date of the invasion had been agreed at the Anglo/American conference in Washington in May 1943, a time of very low public confidence and morale. In the ensuing twelve months, after a study of the German coastal defences, the beaches and, of course, the weather patterns, the Operation was scheduled for Monday 5th June 1944. Uncertain conditions in the English Channel and their effect on the landing craft caused a one-day postponement. The landings, involving the use of approximately 4,000 ships, with several thousand smaller craft, were made under cover of the most gigantic air umbrella ever seen. Between midnight and 8.00 am some 31,000 Allied airmen were sent over France, to soften up the German defences. This aerial bombing was supported by a naval bombardment from battleships, cruisers, destroyers, and specially designed close-support vessels. Naval losses and indeed those in the air and on shore were reported as being surprisingly small; the elaborate Allied deception plans having obviously fooled the 'Jerries' – typical British slang reference to their fighting helmets resembling the 'piss pot' resident under most British beds in those days!

The first landings were made during the night when airborne troops of both British and American formations flew in well over 1,000 troop-carrying aircraft and gliders. A remarkable feature of the day's operations was the absence of effective aerial opposition by the Luftwaffe. Five assault points were targeted and given the code names of Utah, Omaha, Gold, Juno, and Sword. The first two of those beachheads were entrusted to the Americans, whilst Gold and Sword were British led with a combined Canadian/British landing at Juno. The Americans found the Utah landing relatively easy but at Omaha they suffered over 4,600 casualties landing amid the greatest concentration of fire on the invasion front. Many of the amphibious tanks that were meant to have led the assault sank before they reached the beach and so left their infantry unsupported by armour. Hundreds of their troops also drowned in the heavy seas before they could escape their infantry harnesses, weighed down by their sixty-eight pounds of military gear. In comparison to the Americans, the British and Canadian assaults went according to plan and were successful. On 12th June, the Allied bridgehead in Normandy became continuous when the American 101st Airborne Division captured Carentan, which commanded the Vire estuary. This closed the last gap in the Allied front between Omaha and Utah beaches, linking their forces together in a 42-mile wide beachhead.

Whilst the Luftwaffe's bombardment of non-strategic targets, like the homes of us working class and the factories on which we depended for our livelihoods, were unforgivable, little did we know what the German High Command were planning. From sites in the occupied territories across the Channel and the North Sea, the first ever inter-continental ballistic missiles,

East Enders turn out with gifts of food, drink, cigarettes and 'cockney' good luck wishes as a long invasion convoy rolls through the High Street en-route to the docks and to coastal embarkation ports, for transhipment to the assault ships in June 1944. Almost a year later on 9th May 1945, the celebrations for VE Day (Victory in Europe) took place in the same streets and we wondered just how many of those cheerful troops survived D Day, and returned home.

masterminded by the German rocket scientist Von Braun, were about to be unleashed on an unsuspecting public. The comparative rest from the almost continuous bombing endured in 1940 and 1941 was about to be shattered.

On the same night that the Allied forces were linking up on the Normandy beachead, Hitler unleashed the first of his revenge weapons on the civilian 'Home Front', the V-1 flying bomb. The East End took another pounding. This pilot-less plane was launched from sites in occupied France and Holland. Over 9,000 were fired against Southern England between June and September 1944 alone, with Croydon seemingly on their favourite flight-path. Fortunately for us only about a quarter got through the air defences but even so these killed almost 6,200 people and seriously injured about 18,000. In September, as these V-1 launching sites were overrun by the advancing Allies, they gave way to the even more horrific V-2 rockets.

The introduction of the V-1 (or 'doodlebug' as it was nicknamed) between June and September 1944 undid most of our secondary repair work to the previously bomb-damaged homes and came as a sharp reminder that although the Allies were doing well in the Middle East, the Germans still controlled Europe. The indomitable cockney spirit that had been so manifest during the Blitz started to wane and this was further exacerbated when, without warning, the Nazi's launched the V-2. The first V-2 fell in Chiswick with a tremendous detonation heard for miles around. Though a much more expensive weapon than it predecessor, it had a range of about 215 miles but was highly inaccurate in targeting. It was impossible to intercept after launch, climbing as it did to an altitude of about 60 miles and then descending at speeds of up to 2,500 mph. The worst incident occurred across the Thames from us at Lewisham where 160 shoppers died, mostly women and children, when Woolworths received a direct hit. The V-2s caused fear to surge back. With aerial bombing there was at least a warning given. With 'doodlebugs' you could at least see and hear them, but with the V-2 rocket you were either taken unaware when it landed, or killed.

It was impossible to live in such a war torn area without witnessing some harrowing scenes, as people's lives, livelihoods and homes were lost all around us through enemy action. It was an increasingly daily sight to see houses and factories blown apart with tenants' belongings strewn across the streets, left forever as people fled to a safer place. One particular V-2 incident I recall was on a Saturday, around noon. One of the dreaded rockets came out of the skies and exploded onto *The Gog* pub in Freemasons Road, not far from the Victoria Dock. It was filled with workers. I was on the way home from my Saturday morning work, as an apprentice at the local electricity generating station. I was almost half-mile away from the scene when I saw a blinding flash. Then I was almost bowled over by the blast of the explosion and its tremendous roar rang in my ears. Without thinking of the worry that my non-appearance at the expected time might cause my mother, I ran to the scene. I so wish I hadn't. The sight that confronted me was horrific. A once red London trolley-bus had been stripped to its silver aluminium body metal by the blast and its smashed windows revealed graphically to me seated bodies burnt black or mutilated beyond all recognition.

When I eventually arrived home, looking more dishevelled than usual, my mother didn't seem to know whether she should hug me or hit me. She had been in anguish. The dinner was spoiled. Although I could feel my hunger, my mind kept returning to the sickening scenes I had witnessed about an hour before. I had hoped such a wanton and indiscriminate slaughter of innocent civilians would never happen again.

Across the Channel the race was on to destroy the V-2 launching sites before they destroyed the morale back on the 'home front' in Britain, which with the success of D-Day was at its highest point since the war had started. All out air assault, special opperations and the like were made by the Allies to rid us all on the 'Home Front' from the silent and deadly curse of the V2.

Despite the constant menace of the V weapons throughout 1944 and 1945 there was a sense that the tide of the war was turning in Britain's favour and

The main hall of my elementary school – Russell Road, wrecked by a V-1 'flying bomb' on 26th June 1944. This new terror weapon and the subsequent V-2s, launched by the Germans as a 'last throw' to snatch victory from the jaws of defeat, had a far more devastating effect than the Blitz bombs. They destroyed without prior warning, hundreds of homes and factories and caused a large number of civilian casualties.

St Luke's Church in 1971. Opened in 1875 and known as the 'Cathedral of the East End'; it was badly damaged during the Blitz and subsequently repaired. With its 'parishioner friendly' attitude and inspirational Ministers, St Luke's became the focal point of our war-torn community, not only through the Blitz, but from the later bombardment by Hitler's morale damaging secret 'V' weapons.

there was some bizarre easing of tension on the Home Front. The Board of Trade started with the relaxation of regulations of men's clothing. As the Minister explained, 'On the whole we have done something to lift the morale of the country, particularly the morale of the men. The morale of the women has always been high, but that of the men has been depressed by not having enough pockets'. A typical Civil Service view on the things likely to effect the morale of the working class!

High hopes resulted in the Civil Defence outside the London area being virtually disbanded. On the 17th of September, the 'blackout' gave way to a 'dim out', although it remained in force for a distance of 5 miles inland and was briefly and bizarrely re-imposed during the V-2 campaign though God only knows why as these rockets needed no lights to find their targets! On Christmas Day 1944 churches were allowed to light their stained-glass windows and a few days later all public automobiles headlight masks were abolished, probably as by that time there were more civilian deaths on the road, than from Hitler's bombs and rockets.

CHAPTER ELEVEN

From War to Peace – Victory Fires!

By March 1945 it was apparent that Germany was on the brink of collapse. The last of Hitler's not-so-secret 'V' weapons, which he hoped would turn the tide back in his favour, landed in Kent at the end of the month. By April there was a rush to buy flags and bunting as the big department stores like Gamages and Selfridges were besieged by people willing to pay up to 30s (£1.50) for a large Union Jack banner with either 'God Save the King' or for the returning heroes 'Welcome Home' inscribed upon it.

Field Marshall Montgomery, the Allied Commander-in-Chief of the Allied Land Forces (under the Supreme Allied Commander, General Eisenhower) met the German Generals at Luneberg Heath on 5th May to discuss surrender terms, but they were only prepared to surrender those three armies which were then in full retreat in the face of the Russian advance. Monty told them that if those three beaten armies wanted to surrender then it would have to be to the feared Russians! The Generals, acting for Admiral Doenitz who had by then succeeded the reportedly dead Adolf Hitler, refused to surrender those armies facing the Allies. An up-to-date battle map showing the progress of the Allies in the West and the Russians in the East was produced and shocked the Generals who were sent packing to their superiors with the words of Monty ringing in their ears: he would accept nothing less than unconditional surrender. At 1700 hours they returned with complete acceptance of the unconditional surrender terms. The war in the West was finally over when the German Officers put their signatures to the formal surrender document at 1825 hours.

Yet the ordinary man-in-the-street didn't know when the war was actually going to end or if it had ended already. For at least a week before it became fact we expected the announcement of peace almost hourly. On 7th May anticipation mounted and large crowds gathered outside Buckingham Palace scanning the windows and Royal balcony looking intently for any sign of the King appearing, to declare that the war was over. They eventually dispersed as rumours abounded and people began to wonder if the *Daily Express* headline on 2nd May, declaring 'Hitler is DEAD!' was merely a propaganda tool to boost morale.

At last, at around 1940 hours, the Ministry of Information issued a radio statement which put the nation out of its misery which in true civil service style simply said, 'In accordance with arrangements between the three great powers (USA, Russia and Great Britain), an official announcement will be broadcast by the Prime Minister at 3 pm tomorrow, Tuesday afternoon, 8th May. In view of this fact, tomorrow, Tuesday, will be treated as Victory-in-Europe Day and will be regarded as a holiday. His Majesty the King will broadcast to the people of the British Empire and Commonwealth tomorrow, Tuesday, at 9 pm'.

On the following day, 9th May, Prime Minister Winston Churchill, complete with his signature cigar, appeared in Whitehall to what he described as the greatest reception of his career. In his usual slow strong voice he declared, 'God bless you all. This is your victory. Victory of the cause of freedom in every land. In all our long history we have never seen a greater day than this. Every one has done their bit. Every one has tried. Neither the long years, nor the dangers, nor the fierce attacks of the enemy have in any way weakened the independent resolve of the British nation. God bless you all'. And so it was all, finally, over.

This news came as a great relief after almost six years of conflict. It meant the end of the bombing and the return of the servicemen and women and, hopefully, a return to a normal life. Houses could be repaired to a more permanent and decent living standard. Windows and roofing could also be finally replaced with at least a degree of confidence it would remain. People could go to the cinema without the dreaded announcement flashing up on the screen of 'An air-raid is in progress', usually followed immediately by shrapnel being heard striking the roof. Street lamps started to come on again as the blackout was lifted; the protective anti-blast netting stuck on the bus and train windows was removed so allowing passengers after four years to now see where they were going and which stop they were at. The barrage balloon, ack-ack gun and rocket sites were dismantled as were the emergency water supply tanks at some street corners. Fire-watching duties at one's workplace were ended, which was not good news for all men; now there were no excuses for husbands to be out all night!

Celebrations were hastily organised; all were lively and joyous but most of them were spiritless (in the alcoholic sense of the word). The churches were full as everybody, regardless of their religious beliefs, wanting to give thanks for their safe deliverance from the ravages of the Blitz. It was remembered that only a year prior to VE Day, we had seen the D-Day build up through our streets en-route to the docks for transhipment to the assault ships. I vividly recall the Canadian and Colonial British soldiers laughing and joking with us, taking pity on the people and children of the Blitz. Most were very glad they were in the Army rather than being a civilian living in our war-torn streets, having been at the mercy of the Luftwaffe night after night. In his Sunday Service of Thanksgiving our local Vicar recalled their presence at our humble docklands Mission Church in those tense pre-invasion days and sobered our joy and celebration with the thought at how many of those temporary visiting soldiers had eventually returned home. Even as bad as it was, we civilians were glad to have fought our campaign from our home, or what there was left of it and a number of our loved ones around us.

Street parties were hastily arranged even though many of the road's surfaces were unfit through being pot-holed or debris littered. In our road there were just thirteen bomb blasted houses left standing out of over two hundred! So a VE party in South Molton Road was out of the question. However, not to be denied, we street urchins, now in our early teens and having graduated in inventiveness through our Blitz 'education', were determined to make up for lost time with at least four Guy Fawkes Nights! We set about having the most enormous street bonfire of all time. Achieving this was made easy for us by the abundance of wood from the bomb wrecked houses plus three old horse-drawn haulage carts from the nearby Fox's Hauliers yard, whose stables had been completely devastated. All its horses had been killed or badly injured in a frightening and unforgettable night raid. Now the carts came in useful once again if only fleetingly!

The amount of wood which we managed to scavenge from the bombed out wreckage of hundreds of homes in the local area, together with a number of disused carts, gave us a bonfire which burnt for three days, threatening to cause as much damage to the street as had the Germans! Finally the Auxilliary Fire Service came and doused our 'flames of victory' but they could not dampen our euphoria or boyish mischeivencies. The thing I remember most about that huge bonfire, was the pyrotechnics which we discovered. We didn't have fireworks so we used large sheets of asbestos which the war damage repair building teams had used after the Blitz. These had been rendered surplus to requirements when the V-1s and V-2s returned to finish the aerial destruction of our homes leaving large stockpiles of 'schoolboy pyrotechnics' readily to hand and by chance we found that if a fairly large piece of asbestos sheet was laid directly over the centre of the fire then, within minutes, it would explode with a large bang, the inherent danger of this was completely lost on us carefree lads. From the ashes of this monumental bonfire we also salvaged the steel rims of the cart wheels and these extended our pleasure as we tried rolling them around the streets until once again we were thwarted by the Council, who took them away as they had done all the house, school and park railings for scrap during the war; ploughshears into swords or something, they had said.

My most poignant memory of the weeks following VE Day, which appeared to have a marked effect on most people around me, myself included, as it soured the taste of victory, was the graphic news of the Holocaust. This widescale slaughter of innocent victims was discovered by the advancing Allies at places such as Belsen, Auschwitz and Buchenwald, which forever more would be indelibly imprinted on our minds and associated with death. Everyone was encouraged to go to our one and only remaining working cinema, the 'New Imperial', and see shocking film footage coming out of Germany and the 'death camps'. Many people could not bear to watch the cinema newsreels. Many of them were physically sick, as they stared disbelievingly at the Nazi atrocities. The terrible pictures from the German concentration camps, which seemed to go on for weeks in the daily newspapers, had a profound effect upon us all even in the Blitzed landscape of the East End as we realised that in comparison to the terrible injustices and horror suffered by those poor people, our deprivations caused by the nightly bombings, our shortages of food, shelter and clothes, were nothing but a minor inconvenience. We didn't have a house, or new clothers, or dinner, or beer, or a packet of 'fags' but at least we still had our spirit and generally each other.

When I reluctantly went back to my apprentice work at the local electricity generating station in West Ham I was shocked to learn that one of my schoolmates had been killed on the celebration night, having shimmied up a lamp post to fix some bunting and then fallen to his death. For days after the celebrations the acrid stench of smoke filled the air and our bodies and clothes reeked of burning until the next Friday bath-night. We cheered the news that Hitler had died in the Berlin bunker with his mistress, Eva Braun. But at that time I didn't know that a mistress wasn't a school teacher! Our elders doubted the authenticity of the story and thought it likely to be counter-propaganda of the sort we had been subjected to throughout the war by William 'Lord Haw Haw' Joyce. We tried making up Guys but in the form of effigies of Hitler and Goering, but even old clothes at that time of continuing clothes rationing, were hard to come by. We did manage to make fairly representative face masks of Adolf, with his forelock and clipped moustache, and Hermann Goering with his podgy face and umpteen medals on his broad chest, which we made from silver-papered cardboard and milk bottle tops. Hermann, our tormentor for all those nights of the Blitz, got his 'come-uppance' in South Molton Road in the East End. Finally, and very satisfyingly for us Eastenders, he got his just deserts in the War Crimes Court in Nuremberg where he chose a cyanide pill instead of the hangman's noose. We didn't care; our torturer of the Blitz was dead.

On the 6th August 1945, the Americans dropped the first ever atomic bomb on Hiroshima in Japan and followed this up with another on Nagasaki, causing Japan to surrender. The victory over Japan was celebrated on 16th August and called VJ Day, but there was not the same enthusiasm as there had been for VE Day; perhaps it was because we had not been physically touched by it or perhaps we were mentally and physically exhausted. But the atrocities inflicted on our British and Commonwealth troops and civilians in the prison camps and occupied territories by the Japanese, soon became public and a terrible hatred for them that seemed to transcend that which we felt for the Germans, ensued for many years.

Soon after, a General Election in the country was called to replace the war-time government of unity, with unexpected results. Labour triumphed over the ruling Conservatives and so soon after the victory over Germany. This had the effect of casting aside one of the greatest leaders (Winston Churchill) this country has ever known and was seen outside Britain by Allies and enemies alike, as completely unbelievable. As a politically ignorant fifteen year old at the time, I too, did not understand the public's short memory by kicking out such an icon at the height of his and the country's success. However, to many East Enders, Churchill was seen as 'a warmonger'. He had merely reinforced an old working-class belief that the Tories welcomed war as a way of reducing unemployment and a sure way to make the rich richer. The surprise General Election result wasn't, however, a reflection on Churchill and his personal efforts as the nation's saviour, or any question of ingratitude to the great man. It was the fact that most people were poor working class and they had experienced the deprivation of war as a worsening extension on the grim decade of the 1930s and they didn't want to return to it. It wasn't the man that the voters were rejecting; it was the Tory Party and their policies, which had so affected the pre-war man-in-the-street. Thus Clement Attlee became the first Labour Prime Minister with a clear two to one majority, with most of the East End behind him.

However, the new PM inherited many post-war problems. Fighting and winning the war was one thing; delivering the benefits of the peace quite another. The long war had saddled Britain with colossal overseas debts, par-ticularly to the Americans in the Lease Lend payback – the final payments only being discharged in 2007, some sixty-two years later! Britain now faced a 'financial Dunkirk', as many as four million homes, almost a third of the national total, had been bomb damaged, including half-a-million totally destroyed. The war had ended, but the onerous task of reconstructing Britain lay immediately ahead.

As we rejoiced in the euphoria of victory the national cupboard was bare and there very quickly followed the stark realisation that the country had suffered greatly. Roads, schools, hospitals, factories, the docks and factories of the East End all needed rebuilding. As a result, the belts, which we were told to tighten in the very darkest and bleakest days of war, would now not be relaxed as we had all dreamt. Shortages of almost everything remained. The cinema and theatre lights which had dazzled us all on VE Night had been switched off again, not to save us from the Luftwaffe bomb aimer's sights but in order now to save fuel. There was less meat in the shops than there had been the year before. In May the bacon ration had been further reduced and in the September of the Victory Year, the clothing ration was cut once again. Even bread was rationed.

Among the most significant acts of the new Labour Government was a free health service for everybody and only those who have lived between-war

years can really appreciate the social revolution brought about by this legislation. Before the NHS was established, people had to pay a national health
stamp out of their wages. This entitled a person to be registered with a
doctor, but only you could get a doctor for free. If you were married; the
wife and family had to be paid for. Some employers had a penny-a-week
health insurance scheme, which covered the worker's family with an
appointed doctor, but most had no health cover and many suffered as a result.

To indemnify families who could ill-afford to pay for a hospital stay, many
belonged to the 3*d* (thruppence) a week Hospital Savings Association (HSA),
but this scheme did not cover visits to the doctor. At less than one year old I
had the misfortune to contract diphtheria, which put me in a life-threatening
situation. I was rushed into Samson Street Fever Hospital. My mother had
to pay for this; heaven knows how she afforded it from my dad's meagre
seagoing wages. Later I recall, before the new NHS, my mother would
always take 2*s* (two shillings) when she took me to the doctors, to pay for a
certificate and a prescription.

With men returning from the forces to a 'land fit for heroes' there was fierce
competition for jobs. This was amply demonstrated in the East End outside
the dock gates. Most mornings I witnessed large gatherings of men waiting to
be picked for 'piecework', but if your 'face didn't fit', you didn't get work.
With the wartime increase in shipbuilding the size of cargo ships had increased
dramatically such that the Royal Docks or the Thames Docks were now not
big enough for the increase in ship sizes. Some ships took a whole day to come
down river, queue through the locks and almost a day to dock. Time was
money, and gradually the docks sadly closed as shipping was transferred to
larger coastal ports. The closures were also accelerated by the introduction of
a dock labour scheme where everyone earned the same and 'piecework' rates
were no longer paid. This forced employers to take on a certain number of
men without enough to do, resulting in those 'working their guts out' getting
only the same as those sent home; so causing disharmony and strikes. The
local joke was that Dockers didn't save to go on holiday, they saved to go on
strike. In retrospect I'm glad I became a Clerk.

Some semblance of day to day normality had already begun to return after
the Allied advance through France & the Low Counties had destroyed the
German V-1 and V-2 launching sites in late 1944, thus removing finally
the threat of obliteration to us East Enders. Throughout the darkest days of
the Blitz and later the 'doodlebugs' and V-rockets, the rallying cry of 'London
can take it!' had been regularly heard, though fear and fatigue had been felt
by all who had lived through those almost continuous attacks. The relief of
survival showed clearly on harrowed faces all around. My family had fared
much better than many others around us who had lost not only their homes
and belongings, but loved ones, either by German bombing on the mainland

or by enemy action on the battlefront. But despite being physically unscathed, the mental scars were raw for us all.

In 1945, after four years of mental decline, my only sister was diagnosed epileptic and brain damaged as a result of one of the heavy air raids when she was just six. I have no memory of why, but on that particular night raid, my mother, sister and myself were sheltering under the kitchen table when a large bomb exploded quite near to us and the rest of our kitchen ceiling came crashing down, causing my sister to scream non-stop and shake uncontrollably. At that time (1941), she was unable to receive the appropriate medical treatment for her obvious oncoming handicap, so that over the ensuing sixty-odd years, she has never received an education or worked. Now registered disabled, she is a permanent resident in a care home and has been so since my mother's death in 1992. Another casualty of the Blitz.

Dad stayed at sea until after the end of the Second World War, by which time he had risen to the rank of Head Chef in the Union Castle Lines on the South Africa run. In late 1945 he said his sad farewells to his sea-going life to take his place as full time dad. For the first time in about thirty years, he began working on land, taking a cooking job in a post-war rebuilding construction company. They had established a large labour camp literally yards away from where we lived in our bomb-ravaged house and road. Before retiring in the mid-1960s he worked for the local Lamson Paragon, a large commercial printing firm, followed by a few years at the American Sackville Club in the West End. In all his working life, I never heard my father complain about his job or lack of money. Whilst my mother had become an astute businesswoman who knew how to make money but not spend it, my dad never had money but always knew how to lend it and he was content in retirement with his roll-up fags and a 'wee drop of whisky', often secreted around the house in strategic locations such as the outhouse, scullery or under the stairs. What he never knew was mum's 'secret' marking of his bottles so she could track his drinking!

The war had changed the face of my home, West Ham forever. Mass evacuations followed by the devastating aerial bombardment by the Luftwaffe and the V-1 and V-2 pilotless missiles had destroyed and further depopulated our tough community. However, out of the hardship of being 'soldiers of the front line' and from the continuing poverty and overcrowded conditions, an enduring spirit emerged which came to characterise a 'West Hammer', known for their gritty, down-to-earth attitude that bonded neighbours and families through mutual support and shared memories.

Major rebuilding followed the post-war years and my Borough underwent many changes as old familiar landmarks disappeared and new residents moved in, particularly from the Caribbean and South Asia. Much later in 1965, West Ham and its neighbour East Ham, were amalgamated to form the London Borough of Newham, thus ending our 1,000 year link with Essex.

St Albans Cricket Team, Summer 1947. I am on the front row, second from the right

Speedway: In the summer the 'dirt track' was popular (or 'Speedway' as it was officially named.) West Ham Stadium in Custom House was second only to Wembley in its size for both speedway and greyhound racing, being able to hold over 40,000 people. With 'Bluey' Wilkinson, 'Tiger' Stevenson and Eric Chitty, the team was amongst the best in the country. The Stadium opened in 1928, was closed in September 1940 when the Blitz began, but reopened a few years after the war, before being permanently closed in 1972. A housing estate was built over the site of the stadium with some of its street names commemorating famous speedway stars.

The days when one could leave a front door ajar, windows open or the house keys on a string in the letterbox were gone. Crime rates, particularly among the younger inhabitants, rose alarmingly. Consequently, many of the original pre-war population moved out to Essex, so retaining the old historical links when West Ham was the last place in Essex before London.

The Second World War brought dramatic changes to my home. Thousands of East Enders were evacuated to safer areas or moved away, never to return. The area was one of the most heavily bombed in Britain and many families suffered tragedy. It was not until the early 1960s that many of the remaining bomb sites were replaced by new houses, high rise flats, shops and a street market but over the following decade, many of the long established industries either closed completely, moved away or reduced their workforce as automation overtook the previously abundant manual labour market, drawn from the streets of Canning Town, Poplar, East and West Ham, Upton Park, Silvertown and Stratford.

The Royal Docks, which had provided the base for so much of the area's economic viability, closed in 1981. In an area where work had been available, if one didn't mind the poor working and housing conditions, standards slipped. A sharp rise in unemployment resulted in increased levels of poverty and crime, coupled with deteriorating accommodation and health.

Run-down and neglected, Canning Town was never to return to its former industrial prominence and its contribution to the Country's economy, through manufacturing, imports and exports, is now all but forgotten.

Conscription – Off to the Army

At the end of 1947 it was almost as if the family merry-go-round had come full circle and a new era was about to start with my joining the Army. But unlike my Grandfather, I had no need to run away to Scotland to escape punishment by joining the Argyll & Sutherland Highlanders. I was conscripted (like it or not) into the British Army with the Royal Corps of Signals, for a two-year stint of National Service and spending eighteen months helping maintain a strategic reserve for the potentially volatile area of the Middle East – Egypt in my case.

The first six months of military training, in what was considered to be one of the coldest years since records began, was spent being both bullied and verbally abused by sadistic NCOs clearly intent on breaking one's spirit and proving to themselves that we were the 'Biggest load of s*** to have ever worn the King's uniform!' What with the cold and the regimentation, I would often regret that I survived the German Blitz, so as not to be suffering the humiliation of the abuse that was meted out in the name of discipline! However, in retrospect, it lessened my previous dependence upon my

Me in March 1948, aged 18, as Signalman C. J. Smith of the Royal Corps of Signals.

family, plus giving me a sense of real responsibility and self-reliance and all for twenty-eight shillings a week (£1.40 today). I learned a lot in the Army in those two years, not in the academic sense, but about life, as I discovered myself, gaining confidence with a broader outlook than that which my living in the East End had restricted me to. I went into the Army as a boy, but I like to think that I came out as a man!

Although finishing my National Service commitment at the end of 1949, I was placed on the 'Reservist List' during the first half of the 1950s whilst North Korea and South Korea fought out their differences, with the USA and Britain supporting the non-Communist South. The 1950s saw the first Hydrogen bomb testing, the death of Stalin, the conquest of Mount Everest,

Just wed to new bride Eileen Patricia, daughter of a seagoing colleague of my father, at
St Michaels on the Mount, Welling, Kent, in clean and peaceful post-war suburbia,
4 September 1954.

the coronation of Queen Elizabeth II, the first 'four-minute mile', the first launch into space and my marriage in 1954.

Almost without my knowing, the war had shaped my future and made me appreciate the life and luxuries I now enjoy in my old age. One thing I am certain of though, is having endured the depths of fear, delivered almost nightly by the droning Lufwaffe bombers whilst huddled in the shelter with my grandparents, my mother and sister, whatever life has in store for me, I will never be as terrified again.

Throughout the war years, my grandfather was my surrogate father and I will forever be indebted to him for looking after me when my own father was away at sea. My mother, although loving, was busy trying to supplement the meagre family income by working and reluctantly left me in the good care of indulgent grandparents. From the close relationship I had with my grandfather, I learned the value of laughter in times of worry and unhappiness and I gained an insight into his fascinating and adventurous life. In writing this book, it has made me wonder how all our lives would have been different, had my grandfather not hung up those paper chains in Massie's Bakery and run away from Bootle Docks to a start a new life and a family in London's East End.

Epilogue

From Past Times to Present Times – Life's Reflections

Fast forward now to 7 July 2005. An eagerly awaited worldwide announcement from Singapore regarding the staging of the next Olympic Games in 2012 went something like '. . . and the city which has been selected by the International Olympic Committee to host the 2012 Olympic Games is (then a long and deliberate nail biting pause) . . . London!'

The mounting tension on the back of so many months preparing London's Olympic bid, climaxing in the Singapore announcement, was met with euphoria as wild scenes were screened on TV live from Singapore and the public reaction in the UK. While the Olympic Bid team led by Sebastian Coe, the highly successful British middle distance runner accompanied by East End boy but unfortunately never a West Ham player, David Beckham and Prime Minister Tony Blair, the face of 'New Labour' so distant from the Keir Hardy role model of my grandfather and father's day, were seen dancing jigs around the Singapore hall and punching the air with obvious delight, at home the general public's patriotic fervour manifested itself in Trafalgar Square signalling to a hero of a former time, Lord Nelson, high above, that in this Battle of Trafalgar Anniversary year, once again we had beaten the French! Excitement gripped the nation throughout the afternoon and evening in scenes which reminded me of the 1945 Second World War victory celebrations. London had triumphed over Paris' bid against all the odds and national pride was back on the agenda big time!

This triumphal and euphoric occasion prompted me as one of the ever dwindling 'golden oldies' who were alive and could remember the last time that London hosted the Games, into thinking back to the last London Olympics and about the cataclysmic differences between then and now.

It was 1948, just three years after the war had ended. It was some poetic justice to me having endured all that Hitler could hurl at us and seeing all the destruction around me that my home city, London, should host the first Olympics since the Berlin games. The war had caused a break of twelve years in the Olympic schedule, the last being held in Berlin in 1936, a time when fascism was rearing its ugly head. Hitler wanted the 1936 Games to be an Aryan triumph, a showcase for the Nazis racist doctrine of Nordic supremacy causing the Berlin Games to be infamous for its labelling of the black American team members as 'mercenaries' and 'auxiliaries'. Consequently Hitler not only refused to be photographed with the black American athlete Jesse Owens, winner of four Gold medals in 100, 200 and 4 × 100 metre races and also in the long jump, but left the stadium rather than acknowledge Owen's obvious sporting prowess.

As had been common among the children of pre-war East End days as we indulged in our street games, the names of our 'home grown' sporting heroes were quickly assumed mantles. I remember that we all wanted to be Ted Drake of Arsenal in our street kickabouts or Jack Hobbs of Surrey in our street cricket matches. However, athletics or 'running' as we knew it then, was a branch of sport that was new to us street kids and although Jesse Owens was the new hero of the hour, being American he was very obviously different to us.

We mocked Hitler, the Berlin transgressor, rather than recognizing Olympic sporting heroes of the day, by holding one end of a black comb against our top lip with the left hand pulling our hair down over one eye while giving the raised right arm Nazi salute and shouting 'Heil Hitler!' before dissolving into childish laughter, not until much later in life realising the seriousness.

By the time that London hosted the 1948 Olympic Games, I was serving my National Service in Egypt and without the luxury of a radio or TV, I had to rely on the local Ismalia newspaper for any results. Uppermost in my memories of those Games was the name Fany Blankers-Koen, a thirty-year-old Dutch mother of two doing a 'Jesse Owens' by winning four of the nine Gold medals available to women competitors. On her return to her home city of Amsterdam, her friends and neighbours presented her with a bicycle 'so that she will not have to run so much'! Now athletes make millions and a few even go into politics!

In my latter life nostalgia has been a Godsend as I have been able to look back and remember most clearly such past events and happenings. However, the long term memory improves at the expense of the short term, for example I recall that in 1948 Prince Charles was born and Don Bradman, the famous Australian cricketer played his last test match, but for the life of me I can't remember what I did yesterday or what I had for dinner today!

However, I do remember why I was writing about the award of the 2012 Olympic Games to London! It would be good for the country as a whole with the world's top sportsmen and women and the tourist followers boosting the national economy and pride but personally, I thought about where the focus of the Games was going to be – yes, Stratford! Not the place with the suffix 'on-Avon' and the birthplace of William Shakespeare but my very own Stratford 'in-East End' which had sufferred so much during the Blitz.

At the time of the 2012 Olympic award, little did I dream that in the 70th anniversary year of the devastating German Blitz on London's East End, I would be given a preview tour of the Stratford site to witness the mammoth construction works two years ahead of the opening of the Games. On this occasion I recalled that the selected site was once a worthless and deserted wasteland of one-time Victorian industrial significance literally crying out for redevelopment. Yet here I was touring what was to be the future Olympic Park area and it was here that I learned that the Blitz debris from the demolished homes and factories which blocked our dockland streets, had been cleared and unknowingly dumped to form the foundations for the 30th Olympiad as, once again, like the phoenix rising from the rubble of the wartime destruction, the East End was being regenerated by the building and staging of the world's greatest sporting spectacular!

Now in my eighth decade I understand all too well that nostalgia can rightly be claimed to play a major part in the ample reflective moments afforded by the onset of old age. Underlying this continual spinning of my oft rusty memory wheels is the belief that 'the further backward one looks, then the further forward one can see'. Thus the previous chapters have been an unashamedly nostalgic trip back into the East End of yesteryear seen through the eyes of one very ordinary family; mine. The journey is seemingly one into a time long ago but actually only less than a hundred years. And how things have changed!

As I reflected on the past and perhaps in recounting it at length in the foregoing pages and considered the extent to which they were the 'Good old days!' which often they clearly were not, I inevitably found myself comparing the 'then' and 'now', particularly the widening gulf between the 'have nothing then' to the 'have everything now' society. But taking the broader national view, rather than the individualistic, I remembered the pride in the wartime patriotism of being British but then became sad that seventy-odd years later, we were sliding ever closer to relinquishing our national identity by becoming 'European' or even the 51st State of America.

I thought of many of those things which set us 'British' apart from the rest of the world; those little things that characterise 'Britishness' and though often copied by others, are never equalled. Things like old village pubs and inns with oak beamed ceilings, log fires and hot 'toddies', cricket on the Village Green, *The Archers*, winding country lanes, ducks on village ponds, thatched 'chocolate-box' cottages, church fetes and vicars and local 'Bobbies' on 'sit-up-and-beg' bicycles etc. To these rural images the suburbanites might well add semi-detached houses with their net-curtains, double decker buses, corner shops, newly mown lawns, and well tended gardens. However, on the 'downside' (to use modern terminology) such suburban memories could additionally include homeless beggars, 'renta-mob' protestors, litter, boarded-up shops, tower blocks and the poor unmarried mothers incarcerated within them. And how about the portrayal and publicity of sex and violence in the media, 'lottery fever', 'road rage', 'negative equity', 'stress and trauma counselling', 'satellite telly dishes', 'Royal scandals' and 'political sleaze' etc.?

Whilst we gave the world our native tongue and so many things that are nowadays taken for granted, especially when we go on holiday, like radar and jet-propulsion to name just two, traditional British character is identified by its self-deprecating sense of humour and being tolerant, reserved, cheerful in adversity, having a strong sense of fair-play, prone to 'side with the under-dog' and a 'soft touch'.

By way of a light-hearted summation of 'then' and 'now' I proffer this poetic postscript of life's comparisons:

How Times Have Changed!

In the poor docklands area of London's East-End,
the rich were the 'enemy' and charity our friend.
Secure jobs were scarce and money was tight,
for a day's casual work our Dads had to fight.

Life was much harder and the wages were low,
when I was a boy a long time ago.
In back-to-back houses, two up and two down,
the Landlord was 'King' in our part of town.

No indoor loos, 'cept for the rich titled Gents,
and our bath was a tin 'un, hung on the fence.
No heat or hot water made bath times so hard,
just a cold-water tap and a dash down the yard.

There were no fitted carpets, nor locks on our doors,
but a string on the latch and cold lino' floors.
In down-and-out backstreets though out of a job,
one didn't rob neighbours, 'cos they had nothing to rob.

There were no family cars for the 'working class',
it was walk, bike or tram and no cheap pass!
Never had discos, not that I can recall,
just a radio-gram in a tatty church hall.

No telly, or video or Hi-fi to be had,
only a battery wireless when I was a lad.
A 'night on the town' cost some one-and-a-tanner,
with 'alf a brown ale round the pub's old 'Joanna'.

But all we get now is just 'Karaoke',
gone are the knees up and the old 'Hokey Cokey'
No gardens to sit in then, out front or out back,
just a yard full of junk and coal delivered in a sack.

No washing machines, let alone spin driers,
just Mum and the sink, with wet clothes round the fires.
We never had holidays in lands far away,
only a charabanc trip to 'Sarfend' for the day.

Our family hols were in the hopfields of Kent,
where the few bob hard earned was so readily spent.
New babies came often – NO pill in those days!
Mums were 'oft with child', when Dads had their ways.

Yet we kids were reared without any State Aid,
and clothed and fed, even if the rent wasn't paid.
And when one was poorly, one was seen to at once,
not 'Fill in a form and come back in six months!'

Neither AIDS or Poll Tax or racial tension,
nor the name 'homosexual' did folk ever mention.
No vandals or muggers, graffiti and litter,
that wasn't our 'scene', even if we felt bitter.

Yet we came through the war, 'spite its blackout and Blitz,
so different today with its glamour and glitz.
At old corner shops service came with a smile,
not a cashier's scowl as you line up in file.

Recall how the milkmen, postmen and paper-boys too,
whistled and sang as they delivered to you?
How 'Please' and 'Thank-you' were so feelingly said,
not today's grunt and growl and nod of the head.

We might own our houses and 'get rich' quicker,
but our folks were as happy with just 'alf-a-nicker'.
People seemed happier in those far off days,
much kinder and caring in so many ways.

But I'm not complaining, it's wrong to compare,
life's trials go in circles so we each get a share.
Now I'm old and grey and starting to bald,
I've had a great life, do thank you, dear Lord.

The good times, the bad times, I often recall,
the 'ups' and the 'downs', I've been through 'em all.
Yet I am still smiling – and why should I not?
I'm still healthy and happy with my little lot.

I look at the disabled, the poor and the blind,
then count my own blessings and Dame Fortune so kind.
So when my time is up, how could I complain?
I've enjoyed a great life and would live it again!

Each generation has its time and must give way to the destiny of the next and
to future generations. Such a statement is of course right, but as one reaches

Senior Citizenship this submissive action is more easily said than done, as the older generation conveniently forgets such guidelines and perpetuates the prerogative of the elderly to 'knock' the younger generation. Besides the dominating force of nostalgia in one's twilight years, comes the continual comparisons of two incomparable eras which always results in the same conclusion – 'It's not like it was in my day!' I know, because my grandfather and my father said exactly the same to me when I was part of that younger generation, and no doubt I have said the same to my son as he will to his.

Today's Senior Citizens, 'wrinklies' or OAPs or whatever, were brought up in the days of respect and caring; respect for our elders and other people's property and genuinely caring about and for each other. We lived through the deprivation of wartime food rationing and other shortages, air-raids and often living in run-down or war damaged poor houses, but those were the days when only Field Marshalls and Generals had 'AIDS'; 'pot' was for cooking; 'grass' was for mowing; to be 'gay' was to be happy; 'boobs' were mistakes and 'McDonald's' was a song about farm animals!

Such words like vandalism, hooliganism, racism, sexism and 'joy-riders' were unknown and so had no place in our everyday language. Neither did we hear about 'glue-sniffing', 'one-parenting', 'inner-city riots', 'muggings' and other abhorrent gratuitous violence in the streets and football grounds. We got married first then lived together before we had our children and what we couldn't afford we didn't buy. There were no supermarkets or cash-points, and rarely did a working-class person have a bank account, as the working husbands reluctantly handed over their wage packets on a Friday night to their wives and stood waiting for a hand-back to buy a pint and a packet of five 'Woodbines' or 'Weights'.

Like many of my fellow Senior Citizens, I am sure that the daily dose of news elicits the lament – 'Just what is happening to this country and the younger generation?' Headline news that continually highlights the worst aspects of the society in which we now almost helplessly find ourselves, where murder, the mugging of elderly people and robbery with violence etc., is now so commonplace that it cannot make the front page and is tucked away in the inside pages - if it is reported at all! A society where the perpetrators of crime are given derisory sentences or 'punished' by being sent on exotic holidays with a couple of carers to faraway places (which many law-abiding citizens can only dream about) whilst virtually ignoring the inno-cent victims and their families. No wonder that the 'yob culture' puts 'two fingers up' to the law of the land in open defiance of authority, when the judiciary appear reluctant to impose custodial sentences and the 'softly, softly' approach to justice illustrates often too clearly, that the punishment rarely fits the crime.

As an ex-football fan myself, I deplored the behaviour of some so-called 'fans' travelling abroad to watch England or their local club in European action. I cringed at the newsreels of the beer-bellied skinheads in drunken and riotous scenes heaping more unwanted shame on our country with gross acts offending public decency. This minority element, together with the unruly behaviour of our 'yobs' (who are often 'lad-esses') televised supposedly holidaying in some Spanish, Cypriot or Thai resort, hell-bent on Sun, Sex and Sangria is, unfortunately, seen by many foreigners as representative of the majority of Brits. When I was posted abroad in the Army, it was drummed into us that we were 'ambassadors'; 'So bloody well behave like one, or else!' Today our 'ambassadors' are either representative of a land that no longer endures being educated on the playing fields of some public school for public duty in lands far away or are media aware representatives of the lad-ess 'culture' which so readily emanates from bottles of the latest alcopop brand so readily consumed in copious quantities for the benefit of some fly on the wall documentary for dissemination to an increasingly mindless audience.

In the TV programme *This is Your Life*, so polular in the 1970s and 1980s, so many of the celebrities were only in their 30s or 40s, which I consider to be too young to have had a real life, were feted before an adoring audience of family and friends etc. while viewers were treated, or nauseated, by revelations of what wonderful people they were. At least I waited until I have had what I consider to have been a *life*. As I have qualified for the 'Three-Score-and-Ten' life expectancy stakes I believe I am well qualified to recount my own life.

We had open fires kindled with wood debris from the bombing, toasting forks, curling tongs, wash-boards, gas mantles, trams and very little money to spend, or things to spend it on. Holidays were virtually non-existent unless one went hop-picking, though much later we could go on a cheap-day trip to Southend and 'enjoy' the 'sea' of the Thames Estuary.

Despite the turbulent times we found ourselves in, we had no choice other than to accept what little life had to offer. We were happy but mainly because we knew no different. We didn't know then about the 'I-want-and-must-have-everything' or the 'spend-spend-spend' mentality, now so common in today's society. I happened to be around before TV, micro-waves, Hi-fi, videos, computers, micro-chips, mega-bytes, man-made fibres, ball point pens, fast foods, designer drugs and clothes, pizzas, instant coffee, overpaid footballers and their WAGS!

Provided that the old brain has not deteriorated in direct proportion to one's physical decline, one of the compensations from the attainment of old age status is that of being able to look back and make a self-assessment of one's life – i.e. one's achievements as well as one's failures. The self-criticism arising from that inquest into life's happenings inevitably includes questions like – 'If only I could have my time all over again?' and 'Why did I do that?' etc., while on the self-congratulatory side one might conceivably admit – 'I'm so glad I did that' etc. Whilst there seems to be no one formula for success, I do believe that there is one for failure and that is to try and please everybody. The great

American author, Mark Twain, advised that 'we should all endeavour to lead our lives so that when we die even the undertaker will be sad.' Whilst an admirable guideline, it is an impossible target to achieve as one we all subsequently come to regret.

We humans never learn that the sole purpose of life is to enjoy it. Invariably we have a negative outlook on life believing that happiness is the interval between periods of unhappiness and we have to earn that happiness rather than accept it as a gift to enjoy. In my retrospective appraisal of life's journey with its peaks and troughs of happiness and sadness, I reckon that the Frank Sinatra hit song – 'I did it My Way', adequately sums up my retrospective look at life.

One particular line of an 'Old blue-eyes' song which set my memory wheels spinning was – 'Regrets I have a few, but there again too few to mention . . .'. As I racked my diminishing brain power I couldn't think of any part of my life which I would have changed and so was left with just three regrets viz: I regret *not* having a daughter, *not* learning to play the piano or any other musical instrument and *not* being able to eat and enjoy all types of food.

Among the happier memories of my particular yesteryear are things like Morris Minors (and Morris dancers), 'steam radio' with Dick Barton, Churchill's rousing speeches, Tommy Handley and Vera Lynn, The Crazy Gang, films like *Gone with the Wind* and *Mrs Miniver* and Will Hay and Moore Marriot in *Oh Mr Porter*. Reginald Dixon at the cinema's mighty Wurlitzer, hop-picking and pea-picking, with their almost non-existent basic amenities and safe crime-free and virtually traffic free streets. Most are now truly consigned to history.

The family has entered the third Millennium and the world about us has come a long way. I am left wondering therefore if my father and his father before him, said in their 'one-foot-in-the-grave' situation what I am now saying in mine: 'I'm glad that I am about to leave this increasingly fraught world rather than just coming into it!'

The thought provoking and memory stirring occasioned by my writing this Maudesley family story made me realise how many of John Maudesley's traits I inherited, which helped shape my own life for better or worse. Whilst I am aware of the pride that was so strong in him, finding its way to join the other strong emotions I have about life, I am glad that the one of jealousy did not stick. My philosophy has always been that if you love someone deeply then you trust them just as deeply, so if you are jealous then you don't trust them and, if you don't trust them, you don't love them!

Looking back over my closeness to my grandfather, I feel that his caring and generous nature far outweighed the downside facets of his character. His concern was always for the wellbeing of his family and despite his entrenched views on certain things, there was no doubt in my mind that his heart was certainly in the right place. I will forever be indebted to him for being my

'Dad' during all those years which my own father spent at sea and my mother was busy trying to supplement the meagre family income by working and reluctantly leaving me in the good care of indulgent grandparents.

Isn't it ironic that what I should have told my grandmother and grandfather face-to-face: how much I appreciated them for all that they did for me, is left unsaid for over fifty years after their deaths? I console myself and soften the regret with the thought that they were the last persons who would want praise and thanks for doing 'Only their family duty'.

Fate (see Chapter 2), like John Maudesley talking to that young girl, Kate, in that East End street, plays some funny tricks in our lives, some good and some bad and when I look back on how I came to be me, I always end up with that familiar regret – 'If only . . .', a thought that occurs often, but more particularly at Christmas as I repeat the ritual hanging of chains.

When my son Perry was born, I remember sitting anxiously in the waiting room of the Bursted Woods Maternity Home in suburban Kent and reading a notice on one wall which warned – 'The first few minutes of life are the most dangerous!' and then (in my own light-hearted way) thinking that 'The last few minutes of life ain't all that clever either!'

So, in preparation for my own 'last few minutes' I thought that because of my planning and organising traits, which characterised my life, and having shaken out the 'skeletons' in my own personal cupboard via the foregoing pages, I ought to follow my auto-obituary with a prayer of humility and thanks to my Maker.

Three generations of Smiths: my father, myself and my son Perry
all in our late teens

I set out below, hopefully well in advance of my 'popping off', the kind of prayer that I would like to have said immediately prior to my final curtain call:

The Last Prayer of Charlie Smith

LORD only thou did know me better than I did myself. When I implored you to endow me with Patience you rightly ignored the emphasis of my plea to 'Please hurry!'

I want to thank you dear Lord for trying to keep me from saying something on almost every subject and on every occasion when I often confused 'saying something' with having 'something to say'!

Lord, it must have taken up so much of your precious time as you looked down upon me and realised that the Devil had temporarily distorted the blessing of your gift of life to me by cursing me with only one ear and two mouths!

Thanks be to you Lord for relieving me of the oft-consuming desire of wanting to straighten out everyone's affairs. I appreciated your making me thoughtful but not moody and making me helpful but not overpowering.

With the vast store of knowledge and wonderful memories that thou did bless me with and which will accompany me on the journey to your house, I ask you dear Lord to impart it to those I leave behind in the hope that it will benefit them as it has benefitted me.

Lord I thank you for keeping my tongue relatively free from reciting endless detail by providing me with vocal wings to get to the point.

Thank you for giving me the good grace to listen to others with their tales of woe and their aches and pains, whilst bestowing upon me the ability to endure them with due patience. I was also grateful to you, Lord, for the heavenly sealing of my lips about my own bodily ailments, which though increasing year by year, were made bearable by your allowing me to rehearse such discomfiture in my silent prayers to you.

Whilst I accepted as natural your gift of a good memory, I was aware dear Lord of the growing humility which you instilled in me to reduce my own bigotry, whenever my memory clashed with others, and for teaching me that I could occasionally be mistaken.

Thank you, Lord, for keeping me reasonably sweet and mostly even-tempered. Though I never once aspired to be a Saint (some of them, Heavenly Father, are really so difficult to live with!), neither did I want to become one of your least endearing gifts to mankind, that of ending life as a cantankerous old man.

I am overwhelmingly grateful to you for providing me with the opportunities to have seen and done such wonderful things and to have witnessed the glorious talents of other people but, at the same time, giving me the grace not to be envious of them, but endowing me with the goodness to praise and tell them so.

Though I am ashamed to admit I was but a part-time worshipper in your house, thou knowest dear Lord that in those many times of personal need during my life, I called upon you through prayer, and in return I received your help and guidance on whatever problem was causing me stress and anxiety.

Regretfully, I have not abided by all your Commandments, but hopefully entry into your Kingdom will cause all such earthly sins of mine, which have broken your code of conduct, to be struck from your records.

Lord, whilst I knowingly upheld to the full the unwritten Eleventh Commandment – 'Thou shalt NOT be found out!', thou knowest that in my attempts to grow old (dis)gracefully, you bestowed on me a 'strong Will' but alas, a very 'weak Won't', as I resisted everything but temptation!

I ask you dear Lord, to forgive me my sins and beseech thee not to construe my absences from your Church as an indication of the true depth of my faith. I die a believer and a Christian and thank you for always being at the end of my prayers.

My dying wish dear Lord, is that you open up those Golden Gates and let me enter and enjoy the Glory of the Kingdom of Heaven rather than consigning me to the hotter reception of that place next door! Thanks be to thee O Lord.